OUR AMERICAN HOLIDAYS

THEIR MEANING AND SPIRIT

RETOLD FROM

ST. NICHOLAS MAGAZINE

CHRISTMAS. 1776

Originally Published By The Century Co.
NEW YORK   MCMVI
THE DE VINNE PRESS

2

Originally published in 1906
by The Century Co., New York.

A Better Days Books publication
View the complete Better Days Books
catalog at www.BetterDaysBooks.com

Editorial, sales and distribution, rights and
permission inquiries should be sent via e-mail
to BetterDaysBooks@yahoo.com.

St. Nicholas Magazine/The Century Co.
Our American Holidays/by St. Nicholas
Magazine/The Century Co.

– First Better Days Books Edition.

ISBN 978-1-4357-3140-0

1. Holidays. 2. Christmas. 3. Halloween.
4. Independence Day. 5. Thanksgiving. 6. Easter.
7. New Year's Day. 8. Valentine's Day. 9. America
10. Americana. 11. Title.

CONTENTS

4

PREFACE

To most young people, holidays mean simply freedom from lessons and a good time. All this they should mean—and something more.

It is well to remember, for example, that we owe the pleasure of Thanksgiving to those grateful Pilgrims who gave a feast of thanks for the long-delayed rain that saved their withering crops—a feast of wild turkeys and pumpkin pies, which has been celebrated now for nearly three centuries.

It is most fitting that the same honor paid to Washington's Birthday is now given to that of Lincoln, who is as closely associated with the Civil War as our first President is with the Revolution.

Although the birthdays of the three American poets, Whittier, Lowell, and Longfellow, are not holidays, stories relating to these days are included in this collection as signalizing days to be remembered.

In this book are contained stories bearing on our holidays and annual celebrations, from Hallowe'en to the Fourth of July.

Our American Holidays

If all the year were playing holidays,
To sport would be as tedious as to work.

SHAKESPEARE, *King Henry IV*, Part I.

HO, FOR THE CHRISTMAS TREE!

ST. SATURDAY

BY HENRY JOHNSTONE

Oh, Friday night's the queen of nights, because it ushers in
The Feast of good St. Saturday, when studying is a sin,
When studying is a sin, boys, and we may go to play
Not only in the afternoon, but all the livelong day.

St. Saturday — so legends say — lived in the ages when
The use of leisure still was known and current among men;
Full seldom and full slow he toiled, and even as he wrought
He'd sit him down and rest awhile, immersed in pious
thought.

He loved to fold his good old arms, to cross his good old knees
And in a famous elbow-chair for hours he'd take his ease;
He had a word for old and young, and when the village boys
Came out to play, he'd smile on them and never mind the noise.

So when his time came, honest man, the neighbors all declared
That one of keener intellect could better have been spared;
By young and old his loss was mourned in cottage and in hall,
For if he'd done them little good, he'd done no harm at all.

In time they made a saint of him, and issued a decree —
Since he had loved his ease so well, and been so glad to see
The children frolic round him and to smile upon their play —
That school boys for his sake should have a weekly holiday.

8

They gave his name unto the day, that as the years roll by
His memory might still be green; and that's the reason why
We speak his name with gratitude, and oftener by far
Than that of any other saint in all the calendar.

Then, lads and lassies, great and small, give ear to what I say —
Refrain from work on Saturdays as strictly as you may;
So shall the saint your patron be and prosper all you do —
And when examinations come he'll see you safely through.

HALLOWE'EN

October 31

The Eve of All Saints' Day

This night is known in some places as Nutcrack Night, or Snapapple Night. Supernatural influences are pretended to prevail and hence all kinds of superstitions were formerly connected with it. It is now usually celebrated by children's parties, when certain special games are played.

ALL-HALLOW-EVE MYTHS

By David Brown

As the world grows old and wise, it ceases to believe in many of its superstitions. But, although they are no longer believed in, the customs connected with them do not always die out; they often linger on through centuries, and, from having once been serious religious rites, or something real in the life of the people, they become at last mere children's plays or empty usages, often most zealously enjoyed by those who do not understand their meaning.

All-hallow Eve is now, in our country towns, a time of careless frolic, and of great bonfires, which, I hear, are still kindled on the hill-tops in some places. We also find these fires in England, Scotland, and Ireland, and from their history we learn the meaning of our celebration. Some of you may know that the early inhabitants of Great Britain, Ireland, and parts of France were known as Celts, and that their religion was directed by strange priests called Druids. Three times in the year, on the first of May, for the sowing; at the solstice, June 21st, for the ripening and turn of the year; and on the eve of November 1st, for the harvesting, those mysterious priests of the Celts, the Druids, built fires on the hill-tops in France, Britain, and Ireland, in honor of the sun. At this last festival the

Druids of all the region gathered in their white robes around the stone altar or cairn on the hill-top. Here stood an emblem of the sun, and on the cairn was a sacred fire, which had been kept burning through the year. The Druids formed about the fire, and, at a signal, quenched it, while deep silence rested on the mountains and valleys. Then the new fire gleamed on the cairn, the people in the valley raised a joyous shout, and from hill-top to hill-top other fires answered the sacred flame. On this night, all hearth-fires in the region had been put out, and they were kindled with brands from the sacred fire, which was believed to guard the households through the year.

But the Druids disappeared from their sacred places, the cairns on the hill-tops became the monuments of a dead religion, and Christianity spread to the barbarous inhabitants of France and the British Islands. Yet the people still clung to their old customs, and felt much of the old awe for them. Still they built their fires on the first of May,—at the solstice in June,—and on the eve of November 1st. The church found that it could not all at once separate the people from their old ways, so it gradually turned these ways to its own use, and the harvest festival of the Druids became in the Catholic Calendar the Eve of All Saints, for that is the meaning of the name "All-hallow Eve." In the seventh century, the Pantheon, the ancient Roman temple of all the gods, was consecrated anew to the worship of the Virgin and of all holy martyrs.

By its separation from the solemn character of the Druid festival, All-hallow Eve lost much of its ancient dignity, and became the carnival-night of the year for wild, grotesque rites. As century after century passed by, it came to be spoken of as the time when the magic powers, with which the peasantry, all the world over, filled the wastes and ruins, were supposed to swarm abroad to help or injure men. It was the time when those first dwellers in every land, the fairies, were said to come out from their grots and lurking-places; and in the darkness of the forests and the shadows of old ruins, witches and goblins gathered. In course of time, the hallowing fire came to be considered a protection against these malicious powers. It was a custom in the seventeenth century for the master of a family to carry a lighted torch of straw around his fields, to protect them from evil influence through the year, and as he went he chanted an invocation to the fire. The chief thing which we seek to impress upon your minds in connection with All-hallow Eve is that its curious customs show how no generation of men is altogether separated from earlier generations. Far as we think we are from our uncivilized ancestors, much of what they did and thought has come into our doing and thinking,—with many changes perhaps, under different religious forms, and sometimes in jest where they were in earnest. Still, these customs and observances (of which All-hallow Eve is only one) may be called the piers upon which rests a bridge that spans the wide past between us and the generations that have gone before.

ELECTION DAY

The first Tuesday after the first Monday in November

This day is now a holiday so that every man may have an opportunity to cast his vote. Unlike most other holidays, it does not commemorate an event, but it is a day which has a tremendous meaning if rightly looked upon and rightly used. Its true spirit and significance are well set forth in the following pages. By act of Congress the date for the choosing of Presidential electors is set for the first Tuesday after the first Monday in November in the years when Presidents are elected, and the different States have now nearly all chosen the same day for the election of State officers.

RIGHTS AND DUTIES OF CITIZENS

By S.E. Forman

Read the bill of rights in the constitution of your State and you will find there, set down in plain black and white, the rights which you are to enjoy as an American citizen. This constitution tells you that you have the right to your life, to your liberty, and to the property that you may honestly acquire; that your body, your health and your reputation shall be protected from injury; that you may move freely from place to place unmolested; that you shall not be imprisoned or otherwise punished without a fair trial by an impartial jury; that you may worship God according to the promptings of your own conscience; that you may freely write and speak on any subject providing you do not abuse the privilege; that you may peaceably assemble and petition government for the redress of grievances. These are civil rights. They, together with many others equally dear, are guaranteed by the State and national constitutions, and they belong to all American citizens.

These civil rights, like the air and the sunshine, come to us in these days as a matter of course, but they did not come to our ancestors as a matter of course. To our ancestors rights came as the result of hard-fought battles. The reading of the bill of rights would cause your heart to throb with gratitude did you but know the suffering and sacrifice each right has cost.

Now just as our rights have not been gained without a struggle, so they will not be maintained without a struggle. We may not have to fight with cannon and sword as did our forefathers in the Revolution, but we may be sure that if our liberty is to be preserved there will be fighting of some kind to do. Such precious things as human rights cannot be had for nothing.

One of the hardest battles will be to fulfill the duties which accompany our rights, for every right is accompanied by a duty. If I can hold a man to his contract I ought (*I owe it*) to pay my debts; if I may worship as I please, I ought to refrain from persecuting another on account of his religion; if my property is held sacred, I ought to regard the property of another man as sacred; if the government deals fairly with me and does not oppress me, I ought to deal fairly with it and refuse to cheat it; if I am allowed freedom of speech, I ought not to abuse the privilege; if I have a right to a trial by jury, I ought to respond when I am summoned to serve as a juror; if I have a right to my good name and reputation, I ought not to slander my neighbor; if government shields me from injury, I ought to be ready to take up arms in its defense.

Foremost among the rights of American citizenship is that of going to the polls and casting a ballot. This right of voting is not a civil right; it is a political right which grew out of man's long struggle for his civil rights. While battling with kings and nobles for liberty the people learned to distrust a privileged ruling class. They saw that if their civil rights were to be respected, government must pass into their own hands or into the hands of their chosen agents. Hence they demanded political rights, the right of holding office and of voting at elections.

The suffrage, or the right of voting, is sometimes regarded as a natural right, one that belongs to a person simply because he is a person.

People will say that a man has as much right to vote as he has to acquire property or to defend himself from attack. But this is not a correct view. The right to vote is a *franchise* or privilege which the law gives to such citizens as are thought worthy of possessing it. It is easy to see that everybody cannot be permitted to vote. There must be certain qualifications, certain marks of fitness, required of a citizen before he can be entrusted with the right of suffrage.

But the right of voting, like every other right, has its corresponding duty. No day brings more responsibilities than Election Day. The American voter should regard himself as an officer of government. He is one of the members of the electorate, that vast governing body which consists of all the voters and which possesses supreme political power, controlling all the governments, federal and State and local. This electorate has in its keeping the welfare and the happiness of the American people. When, therefore, the voter takes his place in this governing body, that is, when he enters the polling-booth and presumes to participate in the business of government, he assumes serious responsibilities. In the polling-booth he is a public officer charged with certain duties, and if he fails to discharge these duties properly he may work great injury. What are the duties of a voter in a self-governing country? If an intelligent man will ask himself the question and refer it to his conscience as well as deliberate upon it in his

14

mind, he will conclude that he ought to do the following things:

1. To vote whenever it is his privilege.
2. To try to understand the questions upon which he votes.
3. To learn something about the character and fitness of the candidates for whom he votes.
4. To vote only for honest people for office.
5. To support only honest measures.
6. To give no bribe, direct or indirect, and to receive no bribe, direct or indirect.
7. To place country above party.
8. To recognize the result of the election as the will of the people and therefore as the law.
9. To continue to vote for a righteous although defeated cause as long as there is a reasonable hope of victory.

"The proudest now is but my peer,
The highest not more high;
Today of all the weary year,
A king of men am I.

"Today alike are great and small,
The nameless and the known;
My palace is the people's hall,
The ballot-box my throne!"

--WHITTIER

THANKSGIVING DAY

The Fourth Thursday in November

Thanksgiving is set apart as a day of prayer and rejoicing. The day is of New England origin, the first one being set by Governor Bradford of the Massachusetts colony on December, 1621. President George Washington issued a thanksgiving proclamation for Thursday, December 18, 1777, and again at Valley Forge for May 7, 1778. The Thanksgiving of the present incorporates many of the genial features of Christmas. The feast with the Thanksgiving turkey and pumpkin-pie crowns the day. Even the poorhouse has its turkey.

A THANKSGIVING DINNER THAT FLEW AWAY

By H. Butterworth

"Honk!"

I spun around like a top, looking nervously in every direction. I was familiar with that sound; I had heard it before, during two summer vacations, at the old farm-house on the Cape.

It had been a terror to me. I always put a door, a fence, or a stone wall between me and that sound as speedily as possible. I had just come down from the city to the Cape for my third summer vacation. I had left the cars with my arms full of bundles, and hurried toward Aunt Targood's.

The cottage stood in from the road. There was a long meadow in front of it. In the meadow were two great oaks and some clusters of lilacs. An old, mossy stone wall protected the grounds from the road, and a long walk ran from the old wooden gate to the door.

It was a sunny day, and my heart was light. The orioles were flaming in the old orchards; the bobolinks were tossing themselves about in the long meadows of timothy, daisies, and patches of clover. There was a scent of new-mown hay in the air.

In the distance lay the bay, calm and resplendent, with white sails and specks of boats. Beyond it rose Martha's Vineyard, green and cool and bowery, and at its wharf lay a steamer.

I was, as I said, light-hearted. I was thinking of rides over the sandy roads at the close of the long, bright days; of excursions on the bay; of clam-bakes and picnics.

I was hungry; and before me rose visions of Aunt Targood's fish dinners, roast chickens, berry pies. I was thirsty; but ahead was the old well-sweep, and, behind the cool lattice of the dairy window, were pans of milk in abundance.

I tripped on toward the door with light feet, lugging my bundles and beaded with perspiration, but unmindful of all discomforts in the thought of the bright days and good things in store for me.

"*Honk! Honk!*"

My heart gave a bound!

Where did that sound come from?

Out of a cool cluster of innocent-looking lilac bushes, I saw a dark object cautiously moving. It seemed to have no head. I knew, however, that it had a head. I had seen it; it had seized me once on the previous summer, and I had been in terror of it during all the rest of the season.

I looked down into the irregular grass, and saw the head and a very long neck running along on the ground, propelled by the dark body, like a snake running away from a ball. It was coming toward me, and faster and faster as it approached. I dropped all my bundles.

In a few flying leaps I returned to the road again, and armed myself with a stick from a pile of cord-wood.

"*Honk! Honk! Honk!*"

It was a call of triumph. The head was high in the air now. My enemy moved grandly forward, as became the monarch of the great meadow farm-yard.

I stood with beating heart, after my retreat.

It was Aunt Targood's gander.

How he enjoyed his triumph, and how small and cowardly he made me feel!

"*Honk! Honk! Honk!*"

The geese came out of the lilac bushes, bowing their heads to him in admiration. Then came the goslings—a long procession of awkward, half-feathered things: they appeared equally delighted.

The gander seemed to be telling his admiring audience all about it: how a strange girl with many bundles had attempted to cross the yard; how he had driven her back, and had captured her bundles, and now was monarch of the field. He clapped his wings when he had finished his heroic story, and sent forth such a "*Honk!*" as might have startled a major-general.

Then he, with an air of great dignity and coolness, began to examine my baggage.

Among my effects were several pounds of chocolate caramels, done up in brown paper. Aunt Targood liked caramels, and I had brought her a large supply.

He tore off the wrappers quickly. Bit one. It was good. He began to distribute the bon-bons among the geese, and they, with much liberality and good-will, among the goslings.

This was too much. I ventured through the gate swinging my cord-wood stick.

"*Shoo!*"

He dropped his head on the ground, and drove it down the walk in a lively waddle toward me.

"*Shoo!*"

It was Aunt Targood's voice at the door.

He stopped immediately.

His head was in the air again

"*Shoo!*"

Out came Aunt Targood with her broom.

She always corrected the gander with her broom. If I were to be whipped I should choose a broom—not the stick.

As soon as he beheld the broom he retired, although with much offended pride and dignity, to the lilac bushes; and the geese and goslings followed him.

"Hester, you dear child, come here. I was expecting you, and had been looking out for you, but missed sight of you. I had forgotten all about the gander."

We gathered up the bundles and the caramels. I was light-hearted again.

How cool was the sitting-room, with the woodbine falling about the open windows! Aunt brought me a pitcher of milk and some strawberries; some bread and honey; and a fan.

While I was resting and taking my lunch, I could hear the gander discussing the affairs of the farm-yard with the geese. I did not greatly enjoy the discussion. His tone of voice was very proud, and he did not seem to be speaking well of me. I was suspicious that he did not think me a very brave girl. A young person likes to be spoken well of, even by the gander.

Aunt Targood's gander had been the terror of many well-meaning people, and of some evildoers, for many years. I have seen tramps and pack-peddlers enter the gate, and start on toward the door, when there would sound that ringing warning like a war-blast. "*Honk, Honk!*" and in a few minutes these unwelcome people would be gone. Farm-house boarders from the city would sometimes enter the yard, thinking to draw water by the old well-sweep: in a few minutes it was customary to hear shrieks, and to see women and children flying over the walls, followed by air-rending "*Honks!*" and jubilant cackles from the victorious gander and his admiring family.

"Aunt, what makes you keep that gander, year after year?" said I, one evening, as we were sitting on the lawn before the door. "Is it because he is a kind of a watch-dog, and keeps troublesome people away?"

"No, child, no; I do not wish to keep most people away, not well-behaved people, nor to distress nor annoy any one. The fact is, there is a story about that gander that I do not like to speak of to everyone—something that makes me feel tender toward him; so that if he needs a whipping, I would rather do it. He knows something that no one else knows. I could not have him killed or sent away. You have heard me speak of Nathaniel, my oldest boy?"

"Yes."

"That is his picture in my room, you know. He was a good boy to me. He loved his mother. I loved Nathaniel—you cannot think how much I loved Nathaniel. It was on my account that he went away.

"The farm did not produce enough for us all: Nathaniel, John, and I. We worked hard and had a hard time. One year—that was ten years ago—we were sued for our taxes.

"'Nathaniel,' said I, 'I will go to taking boarders.'

"Then he looked up to me and said (oh, how noble and handsome he appeared to me!):

"'Mother, I will go to sea.'

"'Where?' asked I, in surprise.

"'In a coaster.'

"I turned white. How I felt!

"'You and John can manage the place,' he continued. 'One of the vessels sails next week—Uncle Aaron's; he offers to take me.'

"It seemed best, and he made preparations to go.

"The spring before, Skipper Ben—you have met Skipper Ben—had given me some goose eggs; he had brought them from Canada, and said that they were wild-goose eggs.

"I set them under hens. In four weeks I had three goslings. I took them into the house at first, but afterward made a pen for them out in the yard. I brought them up myself, and one of those goslings is that gander.

"Skipper Ben came over to see me, the day before Nathaniel was to sail. Aaron came with him.

"I said to Aaron:

"'What can I give to Nathaniel to carry to sea with him to make him think of home? Cake, preserves, apples? I haven't got much; I have done all I can for him, poor boy.'

"Brother looked at me curiously, and said:

"'Give him one of those wild geese, and we will fatten it on shipboard and will have it for our Thanksgiving dinner.'

"What brother Aaron said pleased me. The young gander was a noble bird, the handsomest of the lot; and I resolved to keep the geese to kill for my own use and to give *him* to Nathaniel.

"The next morning—it was late in September—I took leave of Nathaniel. I tried to be calm and cheerful and hopeful. I watched him as he went down the walk with the gander struggling under his arms. A stranger would have laughed, but I did not feel like laughing; it was true that the boys who went coasting were usually gone but a few months and came home hardy and happy. But when poverty compels a mother and son to part, after they have been true to each other, and shared their feelings in common, it seems hard, it seems hard—though I do not like to murmur or complain at anything allotted to me.

"I saw him go over the hill. On the top he stopped and held up the gander. He disappeared; yes, my own Nathaniel disappeared. I think of him now as one who disappeared.

"November came—it was a terrible month on the coast that year. Storm followed storm; the sea-faring people talked constantly of wrecks and losses. I could not sleep on the nights of those high winds. I used to lie awake thinking over all the happy hours I had lived with Nathaniel.

"Thanksgiving week came.

"It was full of an Indian-summer brightness after the long storms. The nights were frosty, bright, and calm.

"I could sleep on those calm nights.

"One morning, I thought I heard a strange sound in the woodland pasture. It was like a wild goose. I listened; it was repeated. I was lying in bed. I started up—I thought I had been dreaming.

"On the night before Thanksgiving I went to bed early, being very tired. The moon was full; the air was calm and still. I was thinking of Nathaniel, and I wondered if he would indeed have the gander for his Thanksgiving dinner: if it would be cooked as well as I would have cooked it, and if he would think of me that day.

"I was just going to sleep, when suddenly I heard a sound that made me start up and hold my breath.

"'*Honk!*'

"I thought it was a dream followed by a nervous shock.

"'*Honk! Honk!*'

"There it was again, in the yard. I was surely awake and in my senses.

"I heard the geese cackle.

"'*Honk! Honk! Honk!*'

"I got out of bed and lifted the curtain. It was almost as light as day. Instead of two geese there were three. Had one of the neighbors' geese stolen away?

"I should have thought so, and should not have felt disturbed, but for the reason that none of the neighbors' geese had that peculiar call—that hornlike tone that I had noticed in mine.

"I went out of the door.

"The third goose looked like the very gander I had given Nathaniel. Could it be?

"I did not sleep. I rose early and went to the crib for some corn.

"It was a gander—a 'wild' gander—that had come in the night. He seemed to know me.

"I trembled all over as though I had seen a ghost. I was so faint that I sat down on the meal-chest.

"As I was in that place, a bill pecked against the door. The door opened. The strange gander came hobbling over the crib-stone and went to the corn-bin. He stopped there, looked at me, and gave a sort of glad *"Honk,"* as though he knew me and was glad to see me.

"I was certain that he was the gander I had raised, and that Nathaniel had lifted into the air when he gave me his last recognition from the top of the hill.

"It overcame me. It was Thanksgiving. The church bell would soon be ringing as on Sunday. And here was Nathaniel's Thanksgiving dinner; and brother Aaron's—had it flown away? Where was the vessel?

"Years have passed—ten. You know I waited and waited for my boy to come back. December grew dark with its rainy seas; the snows fell; May lighted up the hills, but the vessel never came back. Nathaniel—my Nathaniel—never returned.

"That gander knows something he could tell me if he could talk. Birds have memories. He remembered the corn-crib—he remembered something else. I wish he *could* talk, poor bird! I wish he could talk. I will never sell him, nor kill him, nor have him abused. *He knows!"*

WHITTIER'S BIRTHDAY

JOHN GREENLEAF WHITTIER

Born December 17, 1807; Died September 7, 1892

Whittier is known not only as a poet, but as a reformer and author. He was a member of the Society of Friends. He attended a New England academy; worked on a farm; taught school in order to afford further education, and at the age of twenty-two edited a paper at Boston. He was a leading opponent of slavery and was several times attacked by mobs on account of his opinions.

THE BOYHOOD OF
JOHN GREENLEAF WHITTIER

By William H. Rideing

The life of Whittier may be read in his poems, and, by putting a note here and a date there, a full autobiography might be compiled from them. His boyhood and youth are depicted in them with such detail that little need be added to make the story complete, and that little, reverently done as it may be, must seem poor in comparison with the poetic beauty of his own revelations.

What more can we do to show his early home than to quote from his own beautiful poem, "Snow-bound?" There the house is pictured for us, inside and out, with all its furnishings; and those who gather around its hearth, inmates and visitors, are set before us so clearly that long after the book has been put away they remain as distinct in the memory as portraits that are visible day after day on the walls of our own homes. He reproduces in his verse the landscapes he saw, the legends of witches and Indians he listened to, the schoolfellows he played with, the voices of the woods and fields, and the round of toil and pleasure in a country boy's life; and in other poems his later life, with its impassioned devotion to freedom and lofty faith, is reflected as lucidly as his youth is in "Snow-bound" and "The Barefoot Boy."

He himself was "The Barefoot Boy," and what Robert Burns said of himself Whittier might repeat: "The poetic genius of my country found me, as the prophetic bard Elijah did Elisha, at the plow, and threw her inspiring mantle over me." He was a farmer's son, born at a time when farm-life in New England was more frugal than it is now, and with no other heritage than the good name and example of parents and kinsmen, in whom simple virtues — thrift, industry, and piety — abounded.

His birthplace still stands near Haverhill, Mass., — a house in one of the hollows of the surrounding hills, little altered from what it was in 1807, the year he was born, when it was already at least a century and a half old.

WHITTIER'S BIRTHPLACE, NEAR HAVERHILL, MASS.

He had no such opportunities for culture as Holmes and Lowell had in their youth. His parents were intelligent and upright people of limited means, who lived in all the simplicity of the Quaker faith, and there was nothing in his early surroundings to encourage and develop a literary taste. Books were scarce, and the twenty volumes on his father's shelves were, with one exception, about Quaker doctrines and Quaker heroes. The exception was a novel, and that was hidden away from the children, for fiction was forbidden fruit. No library or scholarly companionship was within reach; and if his gift had been less than genius, it could never have triumphed over the many disadvantages with which it had to contend. Instead of a poet he would have been a farmer like his forefathers. But literature was a spontaneous impulse with him, as natural as the song of a bird; and he was not wholly dependent on training and opportunity, as he would have been had he possessed mere talent.

Frugal from necessity, the life of the Whittiers was not sordid nor cheerless to him, moreover; and he looks back to it

24

as tenderly as if it had been full of luxuries. It was sweetened
by strong affections, simple tastes, and an unflinching sense of
duty; and in all the members of the household the love of
nature was so genuine that meadow, wood, and river yielded
them all the pleasure they needed, and they scarcely missed
the refinements of art.

Surely there could not be a pleasanter or more homelike
picture than that which the poet has given us of the family on
the night of the great storm when the old house was
snowbound:

> "Shut in from all the world without,
> We sat the clean-winged hearth about,
> Content to let the north wind roar
> In baffled rage at pane and door,
> While the red logs before us beat
> The frost-line back with tropic heat.
> And ever when a louder blast
> Shook beam and rafter as it passed,
> The merrier up its roaring draught
> The great throat of the chimney laughed.
> The house-dog on his paws outspread,
> Laid to the fire his drowsy head;
> The cat's dark silhouette on the wall
> A couchant tiger's seemed to fall,
> And for the winter fireside meet
> Between the andiron's straddling feet
> The mug of cider simmered slow,
> The apples sputtered in a row,
> And close at hand the basket stood
> With nuts from brown October's wood."

For a picture of the poet himself we must turn to the verses in
"The Barefoot Boy," in which he says:

> "O for boyhood's time of June,
> Crowding years in one brief moon,
> When all things I heard or saw,
> Me, their master, waited for.

I was rich in flowers and trees,
Humming-birds and honey-bees;
For my sport the squirrel played,
Plied the snouted mole his spade;
For my taste the blackberry cone
Purpled over hedge and stone;
Laughed the brook for my delight
Through the day and through the night,
Whispering at the garden-wall,
Talked with me from fall to fall;
Mine the sand-rimmed pickerel pond,
Mine the walnut slopes beyond,
Mine on bending orchard trees,
Apples of Hesperides!
Still as my horizon grew,
Larger grew my riches, too;
All the world I saw or knew
Seemed a complex Chinese toy,
Fashioned for a barefoot boy!"

THE OLD SCHOOL-HOUSE, HAVERHILL, MASS.

I doubt if any boy ever rose to intellectual eminence who had fewer opportunities for education than Whittier. He had no such pasturage to browse on as is open to every reader who, by simply reaching them out, can lay his hands on the treasures of English literature. He had to borrow books wherever they could be found among the neighbors who were willing to lend, and he thought nothing of walking several miles for one volume. The only instruction he received was at the district school, which was open a few weeks in midwinter, and at the Haverhill Academy, which he attended two terms of six months each, paying tuition by work in spare hours, and by keeping a small school himself. A feeble spirit would have languished under such disadvantages. But Whittier scarcely refers to them, and instead of begging for pity, he takes them as part of the common lot, and seems to remember only what was beautiful and good in his early life.

Occasionally a stranger knocked at the door of the old homestead in the valley; sometimes it was a distinguished Quaker from abroad, but oftener it was a peddler or some vagabond begging for food, which was seldom refused. Once a foreigner came and asked for lodgings for the night—a dark, repulsive man, whose appearance was so much against him that Mrs. Whittier was afraid to admit him. No sooner had she sent him away, however, than she repented. "What if a son of mine was in a strange land?" she thought. The young poet (who was not yet recognized as such) offered to go out in search of him, and presently returned with him, having found him standing in the roadway just as he had been turned away from another house.

JOHN GREENLEAF WHITTIER

"He took his seat with us at the supper-table," says Whittier in one of his prose sketches, "and when we were all gathered around the hearth that cold autumnal evening, he told us, partly by words and partly by gestures, the story of his life and misfortunes, amused us with descriptions of the grape-gatherings and festivals of his sunny clime, edified my mother with a recipe for making bread of chestnuts, and in the morning, when, after breakfast, his dark sallow face lighted up, and his fierce eyes moistened with grateful emotion as in his own silvery Tuscan accent he poured out his thanks, we marveled at the fears which had so nearly closed our doors against him, and as he departed we all felt that he had left with us the blessing of the poor."

Another guest came to the house one day. It was a vagrant old Scotchman, who, when he had been treated to bread and cheese and cider, sang some of the songs of Robert Burns, which Whittier then heard for the first time, and which he never forgot. Coming to him thus as songs reached the people before printing was invented, through gleemen and minstrels, their sweetness lingered in his ears, and he soon found himself singing in the same strain. Some of his earliest inspirations were drawn from Burns, and he tells us of his joy when one day, after the visit of the old Scotchman, his schoolmaster loaned him a copy of that poet's works. "I began to make rhymes myself, and to imagine stories and adventures," he says in his simple way.

Indeed, he began to rhyme very early and kept his gift a secret from all, except his oldest sister, fearing that his father, who was a prosaic man, would think that he was wasting time. He wrote under the fence, in the attic, in the barn—wherever he could escape observation; and as pen and ink were not always available, he sometimes used chalk, and even charcoal. Great was the surprise of the family when some of his verses were unearthed, literally unearthed, from under a heap of rubbish in a garret; but his father frowned upon these evidences of the bent of his mind, not out of unkindness, but because he doubted the sufficiency of the boy's education for a literary life, and did not wish to inspire him with hopes which might never be fulfilled.

His sister had faith in him, nevertheless, and, without his knowledge, she sent one of his poems to the editor of *The Free Press*, a newspaper published in Newburyport. Whittier was helping his father to repair a stone wall by the roadside when the carrier flung a copy of the paper to him, and, unconscious that anything of his was in it, he opened it and glanced up and down the columns. His eyes fell on some verses called "The Exile's Departure."

"Fond scenes, which delighted my youthful existence,
With feelings of sorrow I bid ye adieu —
A lasting adieu; for now, dim in the distance,
The shores of Hibernia recede from my view.
Farewell to the cliffs, tempest-beaten and gray,
Which guard the loved shores of my own native land;
Farewell to the village and sail-shadowed bay,
The forest-crowned hill and the water-washed strand."

His eyes swam; it was his own poem, the first he ever had in print.

WHITTIER'S STUDY AT AMESBURY, MASS.

"What is the matter with thee?" his father demanded, seeing how dazed he was; but, though he resumed his work on the wall, he could not speak, and he had to steal a glance at the paper again and again, before he could convince himself that he was not dreaming. Sure enough, the poem was there with his initial at the foot of it,—"W., Haverhill, June 1st, 1826,"— and, better still, this editorial notice: "If 'W.,' at Haverhill, will continue to favor us with pieces beautiful as the one inserted in our poetical department of to-day, we shall esteem it a favor."

Fame never passes true genius by, and when it came it brought with it the love and reverence of thousands, who recognize in Whittier a nature abounding in patience, unselfishness, and all the sweetness of Christian charity.

The selections from Mr. Whittier's poems contained in this article are included by kind permission of Messrs. Houghton, Mifflin & Co.

CHRISTMAS

December 25

A festival held every year in memory of the birth of Christ. Christmas is essentially a day of rejoicing and thanksgiving and of good will toward others. Many customs older than Christianity mark the festivities. In our country the observance of the day was discouraged in colonial times, and in England in 1643 Parliament abolished the day. Now its celebration is world-wide and by all classes and creeds.

HOW UNCLE SAM OBSERVES CHRISTMAS

By Clifford Howard

Of course Uncle Sam is best acquainted with the good old-fashioned Christmas—the kind we have known all about since we were little bits of children. There are the Christmas trees with their pretty decorations and candles, and the mistletoe and holly and all sorts of evergreens to make the house look bright, while outside the trees are bare, the ground is white with snow, and Jack Frost is prowling around, freezing up the ponds and pinching people's noses. And then there is dear old Santa Claus with his reindeer, galloping about on the night before Christmas, and scrambling down chimneys to fill the stockings that hang in a row by the fireplace.

It is the time of good cheer and happiness and presents for everybody; the time of chiming bells and joyful carols; of turkey and candy and plum-pudding and all the other good things that go to make up a truly merry Christmas. And here and there throughout the country, some of the quaint old customs of our forefathers are still observed at this time, as, for instance, the pretty custom of "Christmas waits" — boys and girls who go about from house to house on Christmas eve, or early Christmas morning, singing carols.

But, aside from the Christmas customs we all know so well, Uncle Sam has many strange and special ways of observing Christmas; for in this big country of his there are many different kinds of people, and they all do not celebrate Christmas in the same way, as you shall see.

IN THE SOUTH

Siss! Bang! Boom! Sky-rockets hissing, crackers snapping, cannons roaring, horns tooting, bells ringing, and youngsters shouting with wild delight. That is the way Christmas begins down South.

It starts at midnight, or even before; and all day long fire-crackers are going off in the streets of every city, town, and village of the South, from Virginia to Louisiana. A Northern boy, waking up suddenly in New Orleans or Mobile or Atlanta, would think he was in the midst of a rousing Fourth-of-July celebration. In some of the towns the brass bands come out and add to the jollity of the day by marching around and playing "My Maryland" and "Dixie"; while the soldier companies parade up and down the streets to the strains of joyous music and fire salutes with cannons and rifles.

CHRISTMAS IN THE SOUTH

To the girls and boys of the South, Christmas is the noisiest and jolliest day of the year. The Fourth of July doesn't compare with it.

Except for the jingle of sleigh-bells and the presence of Jack Frost, a Christmas in the South is in other ways very much like that in the North. The houses are decorated with greens, mistletoe hangs above the doorways, Santa Claus comes down the chimneys and fills the waiting stockings, while Christmas dinner is not complete without the familiar turkey and cranberry sauce, plum puddings and pies.

IN NEW ENGLAND

For a great many years there was no Christmas in New England. The Pilgrims and the Puritans did not believe in such celebrations. In fact, they often made it a special point to do their hardest work on Christmas day, just to show their contempt for what they considered a pagan festival.

During colonial times there was a law in Massachusetts forbidding any one to celebrate Christmas; and if anybody was so rash in those days as to go about tooting a horn and shouting a "Merry Christmas!" he was promptly brought to his senses by being arrested and punished.

CHRISTMAS SPORTS IN NEW ENGLAND

Of course things are very different in New England now, but in many country towns the people still make more of Thanksgiving than they do of Christmas; and there are hundreds of New England men and women still living who knew nothing of Christmas as children—who never hung up their stockings; who never waited for Santa Claus; who never had a tree; who never even had a Christmas present!

Nowadays, however, Christmas in New England is like Christmas anywhere else; but here and there, even now, the effects of the early Puritan ideas may still be seen. In some of the smaller and out-of-the-way towns and villages you will find Christmas trees and evergreens in only a very few of the houses, and in some places — particularly in New Hampshire — one big Christmas tree does for the whole town. This tree is set up in the town hall, and there the children go to get their gifts, which have been hung on the branches by the parents. Sometimes the tree has no decorations — no candles, no popcorn strings, no shiny balls. After the presents are taken off and given to the children, the tree remains perfectly bare. There is usually a short entertainment of recitations and songs, and a speech or two perhaps, and then the little folks, carrying their presents with them, go back to their homes.

IN NEW MEXICO

In certain parts of New Mexico, among the old Spanish settlements, the celebration of Christmas begins more than a week before the day. In the evenings, a party of men and women go together to the house of some friend — a different house being visited each evening. When they arrive, they knock on the door and begin to sing, and when those in the house ask, "Who is there?" they reply, "The Virgin Mary and St. Joseph seek lodgings in your house." At first the inmates of the house refuse to let them in. This is done to carry out the Bible story of Joseph and Mary being unable to find lodgings in Bethlehem. But in a little while the door is opened and the visitors are heartily welcomed. As soon as they enter, they kneel and repeat a short prayer; and when the devotional exercises are concluded, the rest of the evening is spent in merrymaking.

On Christmas Eve the people of the village gather together in some large room or hall and give a solemn little play, commemorating the birthday of the Savior. One end of the room is used as a stage, and this is fitted up to represent the stable and the manger; and the characters in the sacred story of Bethlehem — Mary and Joseph, the shepherds, the wise men, and the angels — are represented in the tableaux, and with a genuine, reverential spirit. Even the poorer people of the town take part in these Christmas plays.

AMONG THE SHAKERS

The Shakers observe Christmas by a dinner at which the men and women both sit down at the same table. This custom of theirs is the thing that serves to make Christmas different from any other day among the Shakers. During all the rest of the year the men and women eat their meals at separate tables. At sunset on Christmas day, after a service in the church, they march to the community-house, where the dinner is waiting. The men sit on one side of the table and the women on the other. At the head sits an old man called the elder, who begins the meal by saying grace, after which each one in turn gets up and, lifting the right hand, says in a solemn voice, "God is love." The dinner is eaten in perfect silence. Not a voice is heard until the meal comes to an end. Then the men and women rise and sing, standing in their places at the table. As the singing proceeds they mark time with their hands and feet. Then their bodies begin to sway from side to side in the peculiar manner that has given this sect its name of Shakers.

When the singing comes to an end, the elder chants a prayer, after which the men and women silently file out and leave the building.

AMONG THE PENNSYLVANIA GERMANS

"You'd better look out, or Pelznickel will catch you!" This is the dire threat held over naughty boys and girls at Christmas-time in some of the country settlements of the Pennsylvania Germans, or Pennsylvania Dutch, as they are often called.

Pelznickel is another name for Santa Claus. But he is not altogether the same old Santa that we welcome so gladly. On Christmas Eve someone in the neighborhood impersonates Pelznickel by dressing up as an old man with a long white beard. Arming himself with a switch and carrying a bag of toys over his shoulder, he goes from house to house, where the children are expecting him.

A VISIT FROM PELZNICKEL

He asks the parents how the little ones have behaved themselves during the year. To each of those who have been good he gives a present from his bag. But—woe betide the naughty ones! These are not only supposed to get no presents, but Pelznickel catches them by the collar and playfully taps them with his switch.

IN PORTO RICO

The Porto Rican boys and girls would be frightened out of their wits if Santa Claus should come to them in a sleigh drawn by reindeer and should try to enter the houses and fill their stockings. Down there, Santa Claus does not need reindeer or any other kind of steeds, for the children say that he just comes flying through the air like a bird. Neither does he bother himself looking for stockings, for such things are not so plentiful in Porto Rico as they are in cooler climates. Instead of stockings, the children use little boxes, which they make themselves. These they place on the roofs and in the courtyards and old Santa Claus drops the gifts into them as he flies around at night with his bag on his back.

He is more generous in Porto Rico than he is anywhere else. He does not come on Christmas Eve only, but is likely to call around every night or two during the week. Each morning, therefore, the little folks run out eagerly to see whether anything more has been left in their boxes during the night.

Christmas in Porto Rico is a church festival of much importance, and the celebration of it is made up chiefly of religious ceremonies intended to commemorate the principal events in the life of the Savior. Beginning with the celebration of his birth, at Christmas-time, the feast-days follow one another in rapid succession. Indeed, it may justly be said that they do not really come to an end until Easter.

BETHLEHEM DAY IN PORTO RICO

One of the most popular of these festival-days is that known as Bethlehem Day. This is celebrated on the 12th of January, in memory of the coming of the Magi. The celebration consists of a procession of children through the streets of the town. The foremost three, dressed in flowing robes to represent the wise men of the East, come riding along on ponies, holding in their hands the gifts for the Infant King; following them come angels and shepherds and flute-players, all represented by children dressed in pretty costumes and carrying garlands of flowers. These processions are among the most picturesque of all Christmas celebrations.

AMONG THE MORAVIANS

For many days before Christmas the Moravian housewives in Bethlehem, Pennsylvania, are busy in their kitchens making good things for the holidays—mint-cakes, pepper-nuts, *Kümmelbrod*, sugar-cake, mince-pies, and, most important of all, large quantities of "Christmas cakes." These Christmas cakes are a kind of ginger cookie, crisp and spicy, and are made according to a recipe known only to the Moravians. They are made in all sorts of curious shapes—birds, horses, bears, lions, fishes, turtles, stars, leaves, and funny little men and women; so that they are not only good to eat, but are ornamental as well, and are often used by the good fathers and mothers as decorations for the "*Putz.*"

Every Moravian family has its *Putz* at Christmas-time. This consists of a Christmas tree surrounded at its base by a miniature landscape made up of moss and greens and make-believe rocks, and adorned with toy houses and tiny fences and trees and all sorts of little animals and toy people.

On Christmas eve a love-feast is held in the church. The greater part of the service is devoted to music, for which the Moravians have always been noted. While the choir is singing, cake and coffee are brought in and served to all the members of the congregation, each one receiving a good-sized bun and a large cup of coffee. Shortly before the end of the meeting lighted wax candles carried on large trays are brought into the church, by men on one side and women on the other, and passed around to the little folks—one for each boy and girl. This is meant to represent the coming of the Light into the world, and is but one of the many beautiful customs observed by the Moravians.

A CHRISTMAS "PUTZ"

IN ALASKA

"Going around with the star" is a popular Christmas custom among some of the natives of Alaska who belong to the Greek Church. A large figure of a star, covered with brightly colored paper, is carried about at night by a procession of men and women and children. They call at the homes of the well-to-do families of the village, marching about from house to house, headed by the star-bearer and two men or boys carrying lanterns on long poles. They are warmly welcomed at each place, and are invited to come in and have some refreshments. After enjoying the cakes and other good things, and singing one or two carols, they take up the star and move on to the next house.

These processions take place each night during Christmas week; but after the second night the star-bearers are followed by men and boys dressed in fantastic clothes, who try to catch the star-men and destroy their stars. This part of the game is supposed to be an imitation of the soldiers of Herod trying to destroy the children of Bethlehem; but these happy folks of Alaska evidently don't think much about its meaning, for they make a great frolic of it. Everybody is full of fun, and the frosty air of the dark winter nights is filled with laughter as men and boys and romping girls chase one another here and there in merry excitement.

IN HAWAII

The natives of Hawaii say that Santa Claus comes over to the islands in a boat. Perhaps he does; it would be a tedious journey for his reindeer to make without stopping from San Francisco to Honolulu. At all events, he gets there by some means or other, for he would not neglect the little folks of those islands away out in the Pacific.

They look for him as eagerly as do the boys and girls in the lands of snow and ice, and although it must almost melt him to get around in that warm climate with his furs on, he never misses a Christmas.

Before the missionaries and the American settlers went to Hawaii, the natives knew nothing about Christmas, but now they all celebrate the day, and do it, of course, in the same way as the Americans who live there. The main difference between Christmas in Honolulu and Christmas in New York is that in Honolulu in December the weather is like June in New York. Birds are warbling in the leafy trees; gardens are overflowing with roses and carnations; fields and mountain slopes are ablaze with color; and a sunny sky smiles dreamily upon the glories of a summer day. In the morning people go to church, and during the day there are sports and games and merry-making of all sorts. The Christmas dinner is eaten out of doors in the shade of the veranda, and everybody is happy and contented.

IN THE PHILIPPINES

"BUENAS PASQUAS!" This is the hearty greeting that comes to the dweller in the Philippines on Christmas morning, and with it, perhaps, an offering of flowers.

CHRISTMAS IN THE PHILIPPINES

The Filipino, like the Porto Rican and all others who have lived under Spanish rule, look upon Christmas as a great religious festival, and one that requires very special attention. On Christmas Eve the churches are open, and the coming of the great day is celebrated by a mass at midnight; and during all of Christmas Day mass is held every hour, so that every one may have an opportunity to attend. Even the popular Christmas customs among the people are nearly all of a religious character, for most of them consist of little plays or dramas founded upon the life of the Savior.

These plays are called *pastores*, and are performed by bands of young men and women, and sometimes mere boys and girls, who go about from village to village and present their simple little plays to expectant audiences at every stopping-place. The visit of the wise men, the flight into Egypt—these and many other incidents as related in the Scriptures are acted in these *pastores*.

NEW YEAR'S DAY

January 1

The custom of celebrating the first day of the year is a very ancient one. The exchange of gifts, the paying of calls, the making of good resolutions for the new year and feasting often characterize the day. The custom of ringing the church bells is of the widest extent.

The old-world custom of sitting up on New Year's eve to see the old year out is still very common.

EXTRACT FROM
"SOCIAL LIFE IN THE COLONIES"

The Century Magazine, July 1885

By Edward Eggleston

New Year's Day was celebrated among the New York Dutch by the calls of the gentlemen on their lady friends; it is perhaps the only distinctly Dutch custom that afterward came into widespread use in the United States. New Year's Day, and the church festivals kept alike by the Dutch and English, brought an intermission of labor to the New York slaves, who gathered in throngs to devote themselves to wild frolics. The Brooklyn fields were crowded with them on New Year's Day, at Easter, at Whitsuntide, or "Prixter," as the Dutch called it, and on "San Claus Day"—the feast of St. Nicholas.

A CHINESE NEW YEAR'S IN CALIFORNIA

By H. H.

The Chinese in California have a week of holiday at their New Year's in February, just as we do between the twenty-fifth of December and the first of January.

In the cities they make a fine display of fire-works. They use barrels full of fire-crackers, and the Chinese boys do not fire them off, as the American boys do, a cracker at a time; they bring out a large box full, or a barrel full, and fire them off package after package, as fast as they can.

In Santa Barbara, where I was during the Chinese New Year's of 1882, we heard the crackers long before we reached Chinatown. After these stopped we went into the houses. Every Chinese family keeps open house on New Year's Day all day long.

There was no family so poor that it did not have something set out for visitors to enjoy. It was amusing to watch the American boys darting about from shop to shop and house to house, coming out with their hands full of things to eat, showing them to each other and comparing notes.

"Oh, let me taste that!" one boy would exclaim on seeing some new thing; and "Where did you get it? Which house gives that?" Then the whole party would race off to make a descent on that house and get some more. I thought it wonderfully hospitable on the part of the Chinese people to let all these American boys run in and out of their houses in that way, and help themselves from the New Year's feast.

Some of the boys were very rude and ill-mannered—little better than street beggars; but the Chinese were polite and generous to them all. The joss-house, where they held their religious services, was a chamber opening out upon an upper balcony. This balcony was hung with lanterns and decorated. The door at the foot of the stairs which led to this chamber stood open all day, and any one who wished could go up and say his prayers in the Chinese fashion. They have slender reeds with tight rolls of brown paper fastened at one end. In front of the family altar they set a box or vase of ashes, on which a little sandalwood is kept burning. When they wish to make a prayer they stick one of the reeds down in these ashes and set the paper on fire. They believe the smoke of the burning paper will carry the prayer up to heaven.

LINCOLN'S BIRTHDAY

February 12

ABRAHAM LINCOLN

Born February 12, 1809; Died April 15, 1865

Lincoln was the sixteenth President of the United States. He was descended from a Quaker family of English origin. He followed various occupations, including those of a farm laborer, a salesman, a merchant, and a surveyor; was admitted to the bar in 1836 and began the practice of law in this year. He was twice elected President, the second time receiving 212 out of 233 electoral votes. He was shot by John Wilkes Booth at Ford's Theater, Washington, April 14, 1865, and died the following day.

ABRAHAM LINCOLN

By Helen Nicolay

Abraham Lincoln was not an ordinary man. He was, in truth, in the language of the poet Lowell, a "new birth of our new soil." His greatness did not consist in growing up on the frontier. An ordinary man would have found on the frontier exactly what he would have found elsewhere — a commonplace life, varying only with the changing ideas and customs of time and place. But for the man with extraordinary powers of mind and body, for one gifted by Nature as Abraham Lincoln was gifted, the pioneer life, with its severe training in self-denial, patience, and industry, developed his character, and fitted him for the great duties of his after life as no other training could have done.

LINCOLN'S HOME AFTER HIS MARRIAGE

His advancement in the astonishing career that carried him from obscurity to world-wide fame — from postmaster of New Salem village to President of the United States, from captain of a backwoods volunteer company to Commander-in-chief of the army and navy — was neither sudden nor accidental nor easy. He was both ambitious and successful, but his ambition was moderate, and his success was slow. And, because his success was slow, it never outgrew either his judgment or his powers. Between the day when he left his father's cabin and launched his canoe on the head waters of the Sangamon River to begin life on his own account, and the day of his first inauguration, lay full thirty years of toil, self-denial, patience; often of effort baffled, of hope deferred; sometimes of bitter disappointment. Even with the natural gift of great genius, it required an average lifetime and faithful, unrelaxing effort to transform the raw country stripling into a fit ruler for this great nation.

Almost every success was balanced — sometimes over-balanced — by a seeming failure. He went into the Black Hawk war a captain, and through no fault of his own came out a private. He rode to the hostile frontier on horseback, and trudged home on foot. His store "winked out." His surveyor's compass and chain, with which he was earning a scanty living, were sold for debt. He was defeated in his first attempts to be nominated for the legislature and for Congress; defeated in his application to be appointed Commissioner of the General Land Office; defeated for the Senate, when he had forty-five votes to begin with, by a man who had only five votes to begin with; defeated again after his joint debates with Douglas; defeated in the nomination for Vice-President, when a favorable nod from half a dozen politicians would have brought him success.

Failures? Not so. Every seeming defeat was a slow success. His was the growth of the oak, and not of Jonah's gourd. He could not become a master workman until he had served a tedious apprenticeship. It was the quarter of a century of reading, thinking, speech-making, and law-making which fitted him to be the chosen champion in the great Lincoln-Douglas debates of 1858. It was the great moral victory won in those debates (although the Senatorship went to Douglas), added to the title "Honest Old Abe," won by truth and manhood among his neighbors during a whole lifetime, that led the people of the United States to trust him with the duties and powers of President.

And when, at last, after thirty years of endeavor, success had beaten down defeat, when Lincoln had been nominated, elected, and inaugurated, came the crowning trial of his faith and constancy. When the people, by free and lawful choice, had placed honor and power in his hands, when his name could convene Congress, approve laws, cause ships to sail and armies to move, there suddenly came upon the government and the nation a fatal paralysis. Honor seemed to dwindle and power to vanish. Was he then, after all, not to be President? Was patriotism dead? Was the Constitution only a bit of waste paper? Was the Union gone?

HOUSE IN WHICH LINCOLN LIVED
WHEN HE WAS ELECTED PRESIDENT

The outlook was indeed grave. There was treason in Congress, treason in the Supreme Court, treason in the army and navy. Confusion and discord were everywhere. To use Mr. Lincoln's forcible figure of speech, sinners were calling the righteous to repentance. Finally the flag, insulted and fired upon, trailed in surrender at Sumter; and then came the humiliation of the riot at Baltimore, and the President for a few days practically a prisoner in the capital of the nation.

PRESIDENT LINCOLN AND TAD

But his apprenticeship had been served, and there was to be no more failure. With faith and justice and generosity he conducted for four long years a war whose frontiers stretched from the Potomac to the Rio Grande; whose soldiers numbered a million men on each side. The labor, the thought, the responsibility, the strain of mind and anguish of soul that he gave to his great task, who can measure? "Here was place for no holiday magistrate, no fair-weather sailor," as Emerson justly said of him. "The new pilot was hurried to the helm in a tornado. In four years—four years of battle days—his endurance, his fertility of resources, his magnanimity, were sorely tried and never found wanting." "By his courage, his justice, his even temper, ... his humanity, he stood a heroic figure in a heroic epoch."

THE LINCOLN MONUMENT AT SPRINGFIELD

What but a lifetime's schooling in disappointment; what but the pioneer's self-reliance and freedom from prejudice; what but the clear mind quick to see natural right and unswerving in its purpose to follow it; what but the steady self-control, the unwarped sympathy, the unbounded charity of this man with spirit so humble and soul so great, could have carried him through the labors he wrought to the victory he attained?

With truth it could be written, "His heart was as great as the world, but there was no room in it to hold the memory of a wrong." So, "with malice toward none, with charity for all, with firmness in the right as God gave him to see the right," he lived and died. We, who have never seen him, yet feel daily the influence of his kindly life, and cherish among our most precious possessions the heritage of his example.

STATUE OF ABRAHAM LINCOLN
BY AUGUSTUS ST. GAUDENS

THE GETTYSBURG ADDRESS

Fourscore and seven years ago our fathers brought forth on this continent a new nation, conceived in liberty, and dedicated to the proposition that all men are created equal.

Now we are engaged in a great civil war, testing whether that nation, or any nation so conceived and so dedicated, can long endure. We are met on a great battle-field of that war. We have come to dedicate a portion of that field as a final resting-place for those who here gave their lives that that nation might live. It is altogether fitting and proper that we should do this.

But, in a larger sense, we cannot dedicate—we cannot consecrate—we cannot hallow this ground. The brave men, living and dead, who struggled here, have consecrated it far above our poor power to add or detract. The world will little note, nor long remember what we say here, but it can never forget what they did here. It is for us, the living, rather, to be dedicated here to the unfinished work which they who fought here have thus far so nobly advanced. It is rather for us to be here dedicated to the great task remaining before us—that from these honored dead we take increased devotion to that cause for which they gave the last full measure of devotion; that we here highly resolve that these dead shall not have died in vain; that this nation, under God, shall have a new birth of freedom; and that government of the people, by the people, for the people, shall not perish from the earth.

The Gettysburg address was delivered by Abraham Lincoln, November 19, 1863, at the dedication of the Gettysburg battle-field as a national cemetery for Union soldiers.

O CAPTAIN! MY CAPTAIN!

O captain. My captain. Our fearful trip is done;
The ship has weathered every rack, the prize we sought is won;
The port is near, the bells I hear, the people all exulting,
While follow eyes the steady keel, the vessel grim and daring:
But O heart! Heart! Heart!
Leave you not the little spot,
Where on the deck my captain lies,
Fallen cold and dead.

O captain. My captain. Rise up and hear the bells;
Rise up—for you the flag is flung—for you the bugle trills;
For you bouquets and ribbon'd wreaths—for you the shores a-
    crowding;
For you they call, the swaying mass, their eager faces turning;
O captain. Dear father.
This arm I push beneath you;
It is some dream that on the deck,
You've fallen cold and dead.

My captain does not answer, his lips are pale and still;
My father does not feel my arm, he has no pulse nor will;
But the ship, the ship is anchor'd safe, its voyage closed and done;
From fearful trip, the victor ship, comes in with object won:
Exult O shores, and ring, O bells.
But I with silent tread,
Walk the spot the captain lies,
Fallen cold and dead.

WALT WHITMAN.

ST. VALENTINE'S DAY

February 14

Custom decrees that on this day the young shall exchange missives in which the love of the sender is told in verses, pictures, and sentiments. No reason beyond a guess can be given to connect St. Valentine with these customs. He was a Christian martyr, about 270 A.D., while the practice of sending valentines had its origin in the heathen worship of Juno. It is Cupid's day, and no boy or girl needs any encouragement to make the most of it.

WHO BEGAN IT?

By Olive Thorne

There's one thing we know positively, that St. Valentine didn't begin this fourteenth of February excitement; but who *did* is a question not so easy to answer. I don't think any one would have begun it if he could have known what the simple customs of his day would have grown into, or could even have imagined the frightful valentines that disgrace our shops today.

It began, for us, with our English ancestors, who used to assemble on the eve of St. Valentine's Day, put the names of all the young maidens promiscuously in a box, and let each bachelor draw one out. The damsel whose name fell to his lot became his valentine for the year. He wore her name in his bosom or on his sleeve, and it was his duty to attend her and protect her. As late as the fifteenth and sixteenth centuries this custom was very popular, even among the upper classes.

But the wiseacres have traced the custom farther back. Some of them think it was begun by the ancient Romans, who had on the fourteenth or fifteenth of February a festival in honor of Lupercus, "the destroyer of wolves"—a wolf-destroyer being quite worthy of honor in those wild days, let me tell you. At this festival it was the custom, among other curious things, to pair off the young men and maidens in the same chance way, and with the same result of a year's attentions.

Even this is not wholly satisfactory. *Who began it among the Romans?* becomes the next interesting question. One old writer says it was brought to Rome from Arcadia sixty years before the Trojan war (which Homer wrote about, you know). I'm sure that's far enough back to satisfy anybody. The same writer also says that the Pope tried to abolish it in the fifth century, but he succeeded only in sending it down to us in the name of St. Valentine instead of Lupercus.

FOR·THIS·WAS·ON·SAINT·VALENTINE'S·DAY·

Our own ancestry in England and Scotland have observed some very funny customs within the last three centuries. At one time valentines were fashionable among the nobility, and, while still selected by lot, it became the duty of a gentleman to give to the lady who fell to his lot a handsome present. Pieces of jewelry costing thousands of dollars were not unusual, though smaller things, as gloves, were more common.

There was a tradition among the country people that every bird chose its mate on Valentine's Day; and at one time it was the custom for young folks to go out before daylight on that morning and try to catch an owl and two sparrows in a net. If they succeeded, it was a good omen, and entitled them to gifts from the villagers. Another fashion among them was to write the valentine, tie it to an apple or orange, and steal up to the house of the chosen one in the evening, open the door quietly, and throw it in.

Those were the days of charms, and of course the rural maidens had a sure and infallible charm foretelling the future husband. On the eve of St. Valentine's Day, the anxious damsel prepared for sleep by pinning to her pillow five bay leaves, one at each corner and one in the middle (which must have been delightful to sleep on, by the way). If she dreamed of her sweetheart, she was sure to marry him before the end of the year.

But to make it a sure thing, the candidate for matrimony must boil an egg hard, take out the yolk, and fill its place with salt. Just before going to bed, she must eat egg, salt, shell and all, and neither speak nor drink after it. If that wouldn't insure her a vivid dream, there surely could be no virtue in charms.

Modern valentines, aside from the valuable presents often contained in them, are very pretty things, and they are growing prettier every year, since large business houses spare neither skill nor money in getting them up. The most interesting thing about them, to "grown-ups," is the way they are made; and perhaps even you youngsters, who watch eagerly for the postman, "sinking beneath the load of delicate embarrassments not his own," would like to know how satin and lace and flowers and other dainty things grew into a valentine.

It was no fairy's handiwork. It went through the hands of grimy-looking workmen before it reached your hands.

To be sure, a dreamy artist may have designed it, but a lithographer, with inky fingers, printed the picture part of it; a die-cutter, with sleeves rolled up, made a pattern in steel of the lace-work on the edge; and a dingy-looking pressman, with a paper hat on, stamped the pattern around the picture. Another hard-handed workman rubbed the back of the stamped lace with sand-paper till it came in holes and looked like lace, and not merely like stamped paper; and a row of girls at a common long table put on the colors with stencils, gummed on the hearts and darts and cupids and flowers, and otherwise finished the thing exactly like the pattern before them.

54

You see, the sentiment about a valentine doesn't begin until Tom, Dick, or Harry takes it from the stationer, and writes your name on it.

WASHINGTON'S BIRTHDAY

February 22

GEORGE WASHINGTON

Born February 22, 1732 Died December 14, 1799

Washington was the first President of the United States, and the son of a Virginia planter. He attended school until about sixteen years of age, was engaged in surveying, 1748-51, became an officer in the Continental army, and President in 1789. He was re-elected in 1793. He was preeminent for his sound judgment and perfect self-control. It is said that no act of his public life can be traced to personal caprice, ambition, or resentment.

THE BOYHOOD OF WASHINGTON

By Horace E. Scudder

It was near the shore of the Potomac River, between Pope's Creek and Bridge's Creek, that Augustine Washington lived when his son George was born. The land had been in the family ever since Augustine's grandfather, John Washington, had bought it, when he came over from England in 1657. John Washington was a soldier and a public-spirited man, and so the parish in which he lived—for Virginia was divided into parishes as some other colonies into townships—was named Washington. It is a quiet neighborhood; not a sign remains of the old house, and the only mark of the place is a stone slab, broken and overgrown with weeds and brambles, which lies on a bed of bricks taken from the remnants of the old chimney of the house. It bears the inscription:

Here
The 11th of February, 1732
George Washington
was born

SLAB THAT MARKS THE LOCATION OF
THE HOUSE WHERE WASHINGTON WAS BORN

The English had lately agreed to use the calendar of Pope Gregory, which added eleven days to the reckoning, but people still used the old style as well as the new. By the new style, the birthday was February 22, and that is the day which is now observed. The family into which the child was born consisted of the father and mother, Augustine and Mary Washington, and two boys, Lawrence and Augustine. These were sons of Augustine Washington and a former wife who had died four years before. George Washington was the eldest of the children of Augustine and Mary Washington; he had afterward three brothers and two sisters, but one of the sisters died in infancy.

It was not long after George Washington's birth that the house in which he was born was burned, and as his father was at the time especially interested in some iron-works at a distance, it was determined not to rebuild upon the lonely place. Accordingly Augustine Washington removed his family to a place which he owned in Stafford County, on the banks of the Rappahannock River opposite Fredericksburg. The house is not now standing, but a picture was made of it before it was destroyed. It was, like many Virginia houses of the day, divided into four rooms on a floor, and had great outside chimneys at either end.

Here George Washington spent his childhood. He learned to read, write, and cipher at a small school kept by Hobby, the sexton of the parish church. Among his playmates was Richard Henry Lee, who was afterward a famous Virginian. When the boys grew up, they wrote to each other of grave matters of war and state, but here is the beginning of their correspondence, written when they were nine years old.

"RICHARD HENRY LEE TO GEORGE WASHINGTON:

"Pa brought me two pretty books full of pictures he got them in Alexandria they have pictures of dogs and cats and tigers and elefants and ever so many pretty things cousin bids me send you one of them it has a picture of an elefant and a little

Indian boy on his back like uncle jo's sam pa says if I learn my tasks good he will let uncle jo bring me to see you will you ask your ma to let you come to see me.

"RICHARD HENRY LEE."

"GEORGE WASHINGTON TO RICHARD HENRY LEE:

"DEAR DICKEY I thank you very much for the pretty picture book you gave me. Sam asked me to show him the pictures and I showed him all the pictures in it; and I read to him how the tame elephant took care of the master's little boy, and put him on his back and would not let anybody touch his master's little son. I can read three or four pages sometimes without missing a word. Ma says I may go to see you, and stay all day with you next week if it be not rainy. She says I may ride my pony Hero if Uncle Ben will go with me and lead Hero. I have a little piece of poetry about the picture book you gave me, but I mustn't tell you who wrote the poetry.

"'G.W.'s compliments to R.H.L.,
And likes his book full well,
Henceforth will count him his friend,
And hopes many happy days he may spend.'
"Your good friend,

"GEORGE WASHINGTON.

"I am going to get a whip top soon, and you may see it and whip it."

It looks very much as if Richard Henry sent his letter off just as it was written. I suspect that his correspondent's letter was looked over, corrected, and copied before it was sent. Very possibly Augustine Washington was absent at the time on one of his journeys; but at any rate the boy owed most of his training to his mother, for only two years after this, his father died, and he was left to his mother's care.

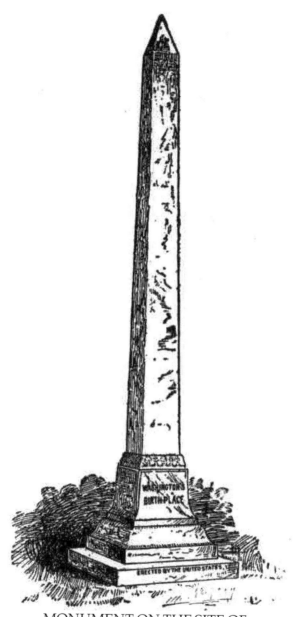

MONUMENT ON THE SITE OF
GEORGE WASHINGTON'S BIRTHPLACE

She was a woman born to command, and since she was left alone with a family and an estate to care for, she took the reins into her own hands, and never gave them up to any one else. She used to drive about in an old-fashioned open chaise, visiting the various parts of her farm, just as a planter would do on horseback. The story is told that she had given an agent directions how to do a piece of work, and he had seen fit to do it differently, because he thought his way a better one. He showed her the improvement.

"And pray," said the lady, "who gave you any exercise of judgment in the matter? I command you, sir; there is nothing left for you but to obey."

In those days, more than now, a boy used very formal language when addressing his mother. He might love her warmly, but he was expected to treat her with a great show of respect. When Washington wrote to his mother, even after he was of age, he began his letter, "Honored Madam," and signed it, "Your dutiful son." This was a part of the manners of the time. It was like the stiff dress which men wore when they paid their respects to others; it was put on for the occasion, and one would have been thought very unmannerly who did not make a marked difference between his every-day dress and that which he wore when he went into the presence of his betters. So Washington, when he wrote to his mother, would not say, "Dear Mother."

Such habits as this go deeper than mere forms of speech. I do not suppose that the sons of this lady feared her, but they stood in awe of her, which is quite a different thing.

"We were all as mute as mice, when in her presence," says one of Washington's companions; and common report makes her to have been very much such a woman as her son afterward was a man.

I think that George Washington owed two strong traits to his mother,—a governing spirit, and a spirit of order and method. She taught him many lessons and gave him many rules; but, after all, it was her character shaping his which was most powerful. She taught him to be truthful, but her lessons were not half so forcible as her own truthfulness.

There is a story told of George Washington's boyhood—unfortunately there are not many stories—which is to the point. His father had taken a great deal of pride in his blooded horses, and his mother afterward took great pains to keep the stock pure. She had several young horses that had not yet been broken, and one of them in particular, a sorrel, was extremely spirited. No one had been able to do anything with it, and it was pronounced thoroughly vicious, as people are apt to pronounce horses which they have not learned to master. George was determined to ride this colt, and told his companions that if they would help him catch it, he would ride and tame it.

OLD WHITE CHAPEL, LANCASTER
COUNTY, VIRGINIA, WHERE WASHINGTON
AND HIS MOTHER ATTENDED SERVICE

Early in the morning they set out for the pasture, where the boys managed to surround the sorrel and then to put a bit into its mouth. Washington sprang on its back, the boys dropped the bridle, and away flew the angry animal. Its rider at once began to command; the horse resisted, backing about the field, rearing and plunging. The boys became thoroughly alarmed, but Washington kept his seat, never once losing his self-control or his mastery of the colt. The struggle was a sharp one; when suddenly, as if determined to rid itself of its rider, the creature leaped into the air with a tremendous bound. It was its last. The violence burst a blood-vessel, and the noble horse fell dead.

Before the boys could sufficiently recover to consider how they should extricate themselves from the scrape, they were called to breakfast; and the mistress of the house, knowing that they had been in the fields, began to ask after her stock.

"Pray, young gentlemen," said she, "have you seen my blooded colts in your rambles? I hope they are well taken care of. My favorite, I am told, is as large as his sire."

The boys looked at one another, and no one liked to speak. Of course the mother repeated her question.

"The sorrel is dead, madam," said her son. "I killed him!"

And then he told the whole story. They say that his mother flushed with anger, as her son often used to, and then, like him, controlled herself, and presently said, quietly:

"It is well; but while I regret the loss of my favorite, I rejoice in my son who always speaks the truth."

The story of Washington's killing the blooded colt is of a piece with other stories less particular, which show that he was a very athletic fellow. Of course, when a boy becomes famous, every one likes to remember the wonderful things he did before he was famous, and Washington's playmates, when they grew up, used to show the spot by the Rappahannock near Fredericksburg where he stood and threw a stone to the opposite bank; and at the celebrated Natural Bridge, the arch of which is two hundred feet above the ground, they always tell the visitor that George Washington threw a stone in the air the whole height. He undoubtedly took part in all the sports which were the favorites of his country at that time—he pitched heavy bars, tossed quoits, ran, leaped, and wrestled; for he was a powerful, large-limbed young fellow, and he had a very large and strong hand.

LONGFELLOW'S BIRTHDAY

February 27

HENRY WADSWORTH LONGFELLOW

Born February 27, 1807;Died March 24, 1882

Longfellow graduated at Bowdoin College in 1825; traveled in Europe in 1826; was professor at Bowdoin in 1829-35; again visited Europe 1835-36; and was professor at Harvard College 1836-54. He continued to reside at Cambridge. He is best known and loved for his poems, though he wrote three novels.

LONGFELLOW AND THE CHILDREN

By Lucy Larcom

The poets who love children are the poets whom children love. It is natural that they should care much for each other, because both children and poets look into things in the same way, — simply, with open eyes and hearts, seeing Nature as it is, and finding whatever is lovable and pure in the people who surround them, as flowers may receive back from flowers sweet odors for those which they have given. The little child is born with a poet's heart in him, and the poet has been fitly called "the eternal child."

Not that all children or all poets are alike in this. But of Longfellow we think as of one who has always been fresh and natural in his sympathy for children, one who has loved them as they have loved him.

We wish he had given us more of the memories of his own childhood. One vivid picture of it comes to us in "My Lost Youth," a poem which shows us how everything he saw when a child must have left within him a life-long impression. That boyhood by the sea must have been full of dreams as well as of pictures. The beautiful bay with its green islands, widening out to the Atlantic on the east, and the dim chain of mountains, the highest in New England, lying far away on the northwestern horizon, give his native city a roomy feeling not often experienced in the streets of a town; and the boy-poet must have felt his imagination taking wings there, for many a long flight. So he more than hints to us in his song:

> *"I can see the shadowy lines of its trees,*
> *And catch, in sudden gleams,*
> *The sheen of the far-surrounding seas,*
> *And islands that were the Hesperides*
> *Of all my boyish dreams.*
> *And the burden of that old song,*
> *It murmurs and whispers still:*
> *'A boy's will is the wind's will,*
> *And the thoughts of youth are long, long thoughts.'*
> *"I remember the black wharves and the slips,*
> *And the sea-tides tossing free;*
> *And Spanish sailors with bearded lips,*
> *And the beauty and mystery of the ships,*
> *And the magic of the sea.*
> *And the voice of that wayward song*
> *Is singing and saying still:*
> *'A boy's will is the wind's will,*
> *And the thoughts of youth are long, long thoughts.'"*

Longfellow's earliest volume, "The Voices of the Night," was one of the few books of American poetry that some of us who are now growing old ourselves can remember reading, just as we were emerging from childhood. "The Reaper and the Flowers" and the "Psalm of Life," — I recall the delight with which I used to repeat those poems. The latter, so full of suggestions which a very young person could feel, but only half understand, was for that very reason the more fascinating. It seemed to give glimpses, through opening doors, of that wonderful new world of mankind, where children are always longing to wander freely as men and women. Looking forward and aspiring are among the first occupations of an imaginative child; and the school-boy who declaimed the words:

> *"Lives of great men all remind us*
> *We can make our lives sublime,"*

and the school-girl who read them quietly by herself, felt them, perhaps, no less keenly than the man of thought and experience.

Longfellow has said that—

> *"Sublimity always is simple*
> *Both in sermon and song, a child can seize on its meaning,"*

and the simplicity of his poetry is the reason why children and young people have always loved it; the reason, also, why it has been enjoyed by men and women and children all over the world.

One of his poems which has been the delight of children and grown people alike is the "Village Blacksmith," the first half of which is a description that many a boy might feel as if he could have written himself—if he only had the poet's command of words and rhymes, and the poet's genius! Is not this one of the proofs of a good poem, that it haunts us until it seems as if it had almost grown out of our own mind? How life-like the picture is!—

> *"And children coming home from school*
> *Look in at the open door;*
> *They love to see the flaming forge,*
> *And hear the bellows roar,*
> *And catch the burning sparks that fly*
> *Like chaff from a threshing-floor."*

No wonder the Cambridge children, when the old chestnut-tree that overhung the smithy was cut down, had a memento shaped into a chair from its boughs, to present to him who had made it an immortal tree in his verse! It bore flower and fruit for them a second time in his acknowledgment of the gift; for he told them how—

"There, by the blacksmith's forge, beside the street
Its blossoms, white and sweet,
Enticed the bees, until it seemed alive,
And murmured like a hive.

"And when the wind of autumn, with a shout
Tossed its great arms about,
The shining chestnuts, bursting from the sheath,
Dropped to the ground beneath."

In its own wild, winsome way, the song of "Hiawatha's Childhood" is one of the prettiest fancies in poetry. It is a dream of babyhood in the "forest primeval," with Nature for nurse and teacher; and it makes us feel as if—were the poet's idea only a possibility—it might have been very pleasant to be a savage baby, although we consider it so much better to be civilized.

How Longfellow loved the very little ones can be seen in such verses as the "Hanging of the Crane," and in those earlier lines "To a Child," where the baby on his mother's knee gazes at the painted tiles, shakes his "coral rattle with the silver bells," or escapes through the open door into the old halls where once

"The Father of his country dwelt."

Those verses give us a charming glimpse of the home-life in the historic mansion which is now so rich with poetic, as well as patriotic associations.

How beautiful it was to be let in to that twilight library scene described in the "Children's Hour":

"A sudden rush from the stair-way,
A sudden raid from the hall!
By three doors left unguarded,
They enter my castle wall!

"They climb up into my turret,
O'er the arms and back of my chair;

If I try to escape, they surround me;
They seem to be everywhere."

Afterward, when sorrow and loss had come to the happy home, in the sudden removal of the mother of those merry children, the father who loved them so had a sadder song for them, as he looked onward into their orphaned lives:

"O little feet, that such long years
Must wander on, through hopes and fears,
Must ache and bleed beneath your load,
I, nearer to the wayside inn,
Where toil shall cease, and rest begin,
Am weary, thinking of your road!"

LONGFELLOW'S HOUSE – ONCE WASHINGTON'S
HEADQUARTERS AT CAMBRIDGE

Longfellow loved all children, and had a word for them whenever he met them.

At a concert, going early with her father, a little girl espied Mr. Longfellow sitting alone, and begged that she might go and speak to him. Her father, himself a stranger, took the liberty of introducing his little daughter Edith to the poet.

"Edith?" said Mr. Longfellow, tenderly. "Ah! I have an Edith, too; but *my* baby Edith is twenty years old." And he seated the child beside him, taking her hand in his, and making her promise to come and see him at his house in Cambridge.

"What is the name of your sled, my boy?" he said to a small lad, who came tugging one up the road toward him, on a winter morning.

"It's 'Evange*line*.' Mr. Longfellow wrote 'Evange*line*.' Did you ever see Mr. Longfellow?" answered the little fellow, as he ran by, doubtless wondering at the smile on the face of the pleasant gray-haired gentleman.

Professor Monti, who witnessed the pretty scene, tells the story of a little girl who one Christmas inquired the way to the poet's house, and asked if she could just step inside the yard; and he relates how Mr. Longfellow, being told she was there, went to the door and called her in, and showed her the "old clock on the stairs," and many other interesting things about the house, leaving his little guest with beautiful memories of that Christmas day to carry all through her life. This was characteristic of the poet's hospitality, delicate and courteous and thoughtful to all who crossed his threshold. Many a trembling young girl, frightened at her own boldness in having ventured into his presence, was set at ease by her host in the most genial way; he would make her forget herself in the interesting mementos all about her, devoting himself to her entertainment as if it were the one pleasure of the hour for him to do so.

HENRY WADSWORTH LONGFELLOW

It is often said, and with reason, that we Americans do not think enough of manners—that politeness of behavior which comes from genuine sympathy and a delicate perception of others' feelings. Certainly our young people might look to Mr. Longfellow as a model in this respect. He was a perfect gentleman, in the best sense of that term, always considerate, and quick to see where he might do a kindness, or say a pleasant word.

The celebration of Longfellow's seventy-fifth birthday by school-children all over the country is something that those children must be glad to think of now—glad to remember that the poet knew how much they cared for him and for what he had written. How pleasant that must have been to him! Certainly, as it seems to me, the best tribute that the young people of the country can pay to his memory is to become more familiar with his poems.

We should not wait until a great and good man has left us before giving him honor, or trying to understand what he has done for us. A dreary world ours would be, if there were no poets' songs echoing through it; and we may be proud of our country that it has a poetry of its own, which it is for us to know and possess for ourselves.

Longfellow has said:

> "What the leaves are to the forest
> With light and air and food,
> Ere their sweet and tender juices
> Have been hardened into wood,
> That to the world, are children":

and something like this we may say of his songs. There is in all true poetry a freshness of life which makes the writer of it immortal.

The singer so much beloved has passed from sight, but the music of his voice is in the air, and, listening to it, we know that he cannot die.

"Somewhat back from the village street
Stands the old-fash-ioned country-seat.
Across its antique portico
Tall poplar-trees their shadows throw;
And from its station in the hall
An ancient timepiece says to all,—
'Forever—never!
Never—forever!'"

INAUGURATION DAY

March 4

The date was settled by the old Congress of the Confederation in 1788, when the procedure was established for the election of a President. It was decreed that the Electoral College should meet on the first Wednesday of January, the votes be counted by the House of Representatives on the first Wednesday of February, and the President be inaugurated on the first Wednesday of March. This March date was the 4th. March 4 has been Inauguration Day ever since.

[**Editor's Note:** The ratification of the Twentieth Amendment to the United States Constitution changed the beginning of the President and Vice President's terms to noon on January 20, beginning with Franklin Roosevelt's second term in 1937.

HOW A PRESIDENT IS INAUGURATED

By Clifford Howard

As you will remember, Thomas Jefferson was the first President of our country to be inaugurated at Washington. This took place in the year 1801, when our national capital was not much more than a year old; and you may imagine that the city was a very different-looking place from what it is to-day. But now instead of a straggling town with a few muddy streets and about three thousand inhabitants, Jefferson would find our national capital one of the most beautiful cities on the face of the earth, with a population of nearly three hundred thousand; and on March 4 he would behold a scene such as he never dreamed of. Thousands of flags fly from the house-tops and windows, bright-colored bunting in beautiful designs adorns the great public buildings, all the stores and business houses are gaily decorated with flags and streamers, and everything presents the appearance of a great and glorious holiday, while the streets swarm with the hundreds of thousands of people who have come to the city from all parts of the country to take part in the grand celebration.

Everybody is moving toward Pennsylvania Avenue, where the parade is to march. No, not everybody: some fifty or sixty thousand make their way to the Capitol, so as to get a glimpse of the inauguration exercises that take place on the east portico; and although the ceremonies will not begin until nearly one o'clock, the great space in front of the Capitol is packed with people three hours before that time, some of them having come as early as eight o'clock in the morning to be sure of getting a good view.

Early in the morning Pennsylvania Avenue is cleared of all street-cars, carriages, and bicycles, and no one is allowed to step off the sidewalk. A strong wire rope is stretched along each side of the avenue, so as to prevent people from getting into the street.

Soon every window and balcony along the line is crowded with spectators. Even the roofs are black with people, and small boys may be seen perched among the branches of the trees, or hanging on to the electric-light poles. For a distance of nearly three miles, on each side of the street, people are packed so closely together that it is almost impossible for them to move. In every park and open space along the line large wooden stands have been erected; and these, too, are filled with those who are willing to pay for seats.

As the time for the morning parade draws near, the crowds become restless with eagerness and excitement. Policemen on horseback dash up and down the avenue to see that the road is clear, and every now and then a trooper or messenger in bright uniform gallops past. Suddenly the boom of a cannon is heard. The next moment there comes the distant roll of drums, and then, amid the inspiring music of brass bands and tremendous cheering, the procession appears moving slowly down the avenue on its way to the Capitol. Riding ahead is a squad of mounted police—big, brawny fellows, with glittering brass buttons. After them come the United States troops and naval forces, armed with their rifles and sabers that flash in the sunlight, and marching to the music of the famous Marine Band, while rumbling over the hard, smooth pavement of the avenue come the big cannons drawn by powerful horses. Then appears the chief marshal of the parade on his spirited horse, heading the body-guard of soldiers that surround the open carriage containing the President and the President-elect, sitting side by side. As the carriage, which is drawn by four handsome horses, rolls slowly along with its distinguished occupants, men and boys shout and cheer at the top of their lungs, and throw their hats into the air when their voices give out, while the women and girls wave their handkerchiefs and hurrah with the rest of the crowd. With hat in hand, the President-elect smiles and bows to the right and the left; and with the bands playing and people cheering, handkerchiefs fluttering and flags flying, he arrives at the Capitol a few minutes before noon. Here he meets with another rousing reception from the great mass of people who have been waiting for him for two or three hours; and it requires all the efforts of a small army of police to open the way for him and his party to pass into the Capitol.

GENERAL GEORGE WASHINGTON
ON THE WAY TO HIS INAUGURATION

The House of Representatives is about to adjourn, and many of its members have already come over to the Senate to witness the closing exercises there. Extra chairs and seats have been brought in for them and the many other prominent officials who also have gathered there, including the officers of the army and the navy, the justices of the Supreme Court, the cabinet officers, and the foreign ambassadors and ministers, many of whom are dressed in their gorgeous state robes. According to law, Congress must come to an end at noon; but if the presidential party has not made its appearance when the Senate clock is about to point to twelve, the hands are moved back a few minutes so as to gain time. And before the hands are allowed to get around to twelve, everybody has arrived, everything is in readiness, and the President of the Senate has administered the oath of office to his successor, the new Vice-President of the United States, who at once calls an extra session of the Senate, so that not a moment elapses between the death of one session and the birth of another. Then, after a short prayer by the chaplain and a brief address by the Vice-President, the distinguished people gathered in the Senate form in line, and, headed by a company of newspaper reporters, they march in dignified procession to the rotunda, and thence to the platform on the east front of the Capitol.

The nine justices of the Supreme Court, clothed in their black robes, walk out on the platform first, followed by the President-elect. As soon as the crowd catches sight of him, a deafening shout breaks forth from fifty thousand throats, and, amid the enthusiastic uproar that lasts several minutes, hats and canes, umbrellas and handkerchiefs, are waved aloft or thrown wildly into the air by joyous and patriotic Americans. Removing his hat, the President-elect comes forward, and, turning to the Chief Justice of the United States, takes the oath of office as required by the Constitution. Then comes the inaugural address, which, of course, only those near the platform are able to hear. But the thirty or forty thousand who can't hear the speech are willing to agree with everything that is said, and every little while they shout and cheer and applaud.

THE INAUGURATION OF PRESIDENT GARFIELD

All this time the crowd on the avenue has been patiently waiting for the return of the President. The morning's procession was nothing more than a military escort; now is to come the great feature of the day—the grand inauguration parade. The ceremonies at the Capitol are over at half-past one, and the new President goes at once to the White House, greeted with rousing cheers all along the way, and prepares to review the greatest parade ever seen in the city of Washington. All the morning, companies of soldiers, political clubs, bands, and drum corps have been preparing for the afternoon's march. There are so many thousands who are going to take part in the parade that orders have been given requiring all companies to march in ranks reaching from curb to curb, a distance of one hundred and thirty feet, and to follow one another as closely as possible.

The march is begun a little before two o'clock; and, although the people have been standing on the sidewalks since early morning, they have plenty of enthusiasm left, and they fill the air with their shouts and hurrahs as regiment after regiment of magnificently drilled soldiers and horses marches by.

Even after the electric lamps are lighted, men and horses are still tramping along the avenue, and people are still shouting and the bands playing and flags waving. And all this time the President stands in front of the White House, reviewing the marching thousands as they pass along.

But although the big parade finally comes to an end, the festivities are not yet over. Late into the night the city is brilliantly illuminated by magnificent and wonderful fireworks and powerful electric search-lights that shine from the tops of the tall buildings and light up the great dome of the Capitol and the Washington monument. Then comes the grand inaugural ball. There are over ten thousand people present, and the scene is a glorious and wonderful sight.

It is almost sunrise when the last carriage rolls away, and with the closing of the ball the inauguration festivities end.

EASTER DAY

Easter is the Sunday that follows the first full moon that falls upon or next after the Vernal Equinox . The date on which Easter falls is not the same every year, and the holiday is therefore referred to as a "moveable feast."

This Sunday, when Christian churches celebrate the resurrection of Christ, is one of solemn rejoicing. Coming after the self-denials of Lent and at the beginning of spring, it seems naturally a time of hope and new life. It is the feast of flowers, particularly of lilies, and the name had its origin in a festival in honor of the goddess of spring. The esteem in which it is held is indicated by its ancient title, "The great day."

A SONG OF EASTER

By Celia Thaxter

Sing, children, sing!
And the lily censers swing;
Sing that life and joy are waking and that Death no more is king.
Sing the happy, happy tumult of the slowly brightening Spring;
Sing, little children, sing!

Sing, children, sing!
Winter wild has taken wing.
Fill the air with the sweet tidings till the frosty echoes ring!
Along the eaves the icicles no longer glittering cling;
And the crocus in the garden lifts its bright face to the sun,
And in the meadows softly the brooks begin to run;
And the golden catkins swing
In the warm airs of the Spring;
Sing, little children, sing!

Sing, children, sing!
The lilies white you bring
In the joyous Easter morning for hope are blossoming;
And as the earth her shroud of snow from off her breast doth fling,
So may we cast our fetters off in God's eternal Spring.
So may we find release at last from sorrow and from pain,
So may we find our childhood's calm, delicious dawn again.
Sweet are your eyes, O little ones, that look with smiling grace,
Without a shade of doubt or fear into the Future's face!
Sing, sing in happy chorus, with joyful voices tell
That death is life, and God is good, and all things shall be well;
That bitter days shall cease
In warmth and light and peace, —
That Winter yields to Spring, —
Sing, little children, sing!

"HE SAT DOWN ON THE STEP,
BREATHLESS WITH SURPRISE AND JOY"

THE GENERAL'S EASTER BOX

By Temple Bailey

The General did not look at all as one would expect a general to look. He was short and thick-set and had a red face and a white mustache, and he usually dressed in a gray tweed suit, with a funny Norfolk jacket with a belt, and wore a soft cap pulled down almost to his eye-glasses.

And he always did his own marketing.

That is how he came to know Jimmy.

Jimmy stood at a corner of Old Market and sold little bundles of dried sage and sweet marjoram, and sassafras and cinnamon, and soup-bunches made of bits of vegetables tied together—a bit of parsley and a bit of celery and a bit of carrot and a sprig of summer savory, all for one cent. Then at Christmas-time he displayed wreaths, which he and his little mother made at home, and as the spring came on he brought wild flowers that he picked in the woods.

And that was how he came to know the General.

For one morning, just before Easter, the General came puffing down the outside aisle of Old Market, with his servant behind him with an enormous basket. The General's carriage was drawn up to the curbstone, and the gray horses were dancing little fancy dances over the asphalt street, when all at once Jimmy thrust a bunch of arbutus under the General's very nose.

"Go away, go away," said the General, and trotted down to the carriage door, which a footman held open for him.

But a whiff of fragrance had reached him, and he stopped.

"How much?" he asked.

"Three cents," said Jimmy, in a hoarse voice.

The General looked at the little fellow through his eye-glasses.

"Got a cold?" he inquired gruffly.

"Yes, sir," croaked Jimmy.

"Why don't you stay in the house, then?" growled the General.

"Can't, sir," said Jimmy, cheerfully; "business is business."

The General looked at the little stand where "business" was transacted—at the little rows of dried stuffs, at the small basket of flowers, and at the soup-bunches.

"Humph," he said.

Then his hand went down into his pocket, and he pulled out a lot of change. After that he chose two bunches of sweet, pinky blossoms.

"Two for five, sir," said Jimmy.

"Hum," said the General. "You might give me some parsley and a soup-bunch."

Jimmy wrapped up the green stuff carefully and dropped it into the basket carried by the General's servant.

"Nine cents, sir," he said; and the General handed him a dime and then moved to the next stall, holding the flowers close to his nose.

"You forgot your change," cried Jimmy, and rushed after him with the one cent.

"Keep—" But one look at the honest little face and he changed his sentence.

Thank you, young man," he said, and away he drove.

After that Jimmy looked for the General, and the General for Jimmy. Their transactions were always carried on in a strictly business manner, although, to be sure, the General's modest family of two did not require the unlimited sage and sweet marjoram that were ordered from time to time.

On the Saturday before Easter the little stand was gay with new wares. In little nests of dried grasses lay eggs—Easter eggs, bright pink and blue and purple and mottled. Jimmy had invested in a dozen at forty cents the dozen, and he had hopes of doubling the money, for work surely counted for something, and he and the Little Mother had dyed them.

But somehow people passed them by. Inside of the market there were finer nests, and eggs gilded and lettered, and Jimmy began to feel that his own precious eggs were very dull indeed.

But when the General appeared around the corner, the boy's spirits rose. Here, at any rate, was a good customer.

The General, however, was in a temper. There had been an argument with the fish-man which had left him red in the face and very touchy. So he bought two bunches of arbutus and nothing else.

"Any eggs, sir?" asked Jimmy.

"Eggs?" said the General, looking over the little stand.

"Easter eggs," explained Jimmy.

"I've no use for such things," said the General.

"Oh!" said Jimmy, and in spite of himself his voice trembled. When one is the man of the family, and the Little Mother is sewing for dear life, and her work and the little stand in the market are all that pay the rent and buy food, it is sometimes hard to be brave. But the General did not notice the tremble. Jimmy tried again:

"Any children, sir? Children always like Easter eggs, you know."

"No," said the General; "no one but a son in the Philippines—a son some six feet two in his stockings."

"Any grandchildren, sir?" hopefully.

"Bless my soul," said the General, testily, "what a lot of questions!" And he hurried off to his carriage.

Jimmy felt very forlorn. The General had been his last hope. The eggs were a dead loss.

At last it came time to close up, and he piled all of his wares in a basket. Then he took out a little broom and began to sweep in an orderly way around his little stall. He had a battered old dustpan, and as he carried it out to the street to empty it, he saw a stiff greenish-gray paper sticking out of the dirt. Nothing in the world ever looks exactly like that but an American greenback, and, sure enough, when Jimmy pulled it out it proved to be a ten-dollar bill.

Jimmy sat down on the curb suddenly. His money always came in pennies and nickels and dimes and quarters. The Little Mother sometimes earned a dollar at a time, but never in his whole life had Jimmy possessed a ten-dollar bill.

Think of the possibilities to a little, poor, cold, worried boy. There was two months' rent in that ten-dollar bill—two months in which he would not have to worry over whether there would be a roof over their heads.

Then there was a basket stall in that ten-dollar bill. That had always been his ambition. Some one had told him that baskets sold well in other cities, and not a single person had opened a basket stall in Old Market, and that was Jimmy's chance. Once established, he knew he could earn a good living.

As for ten dollars' worth of groceries and provisions, Jimmy's mind could not grasp such a thing; fifty cents had always been the top limit for a grocery bill.

But—it wasn't Jimmy's ten dollars. Like a flash his dreams tumbled to the ground. There had been many people coming and going through Old Market, but Jimmy knew that the bill was the General's. For the old gentleman had pulled out a roll when he reached for the five cents. Yes, it was the General's; but how to find the General?

Inside the market he found the General's butcher. Yes, the butcher knew the General's address, for he was one of his best customers, and would keep Jimmy's basket while the boy went to the house.

It was a long distance. Jimmy passed rows of great stone mansions, and went through parks, where crocuses and hyacinths were just peeping out.

At last he came to the General's.

A servant answered the ring of the bell.

"Who shall I say?" he inquired loftily. "The General is very busy, y'know."

"Say Jimmy, from the market, please"; and Jimmy sat down on the great hall seat, feeling very much awed with all the magnificence.

"Well, well," said the General, as he came puffing down the stairs. "Well, well, and what do you want?"

"Please, sir, did you drop this?" and Jimmy held out the tightly rolled bill.

"Did I? Well, now, I'm sure I don't know. Perhaps I did, perhaps I did."

"I found it in front of my stall," said Jimmy.

What a strange thing it seemed that the General should not know! Jimmy would have known if he had lost a penny. He began to feel that the General could not have a true idea of *business*.

The General took out a roll of bills. "Let me see," he said. "Here's my market list. Yes, I guess that's mine, sure enough."

"I'm glad I noticed it," said Jimmy, simply. "I came near sweeping it into the street."

"And what can I pay you for your trouble?" asked the General, looking at the boy keenly.

"Well," said Jimmy, stoutly, "you see, business is business, and I had to take my time, and I'd like to get back as soon as I can."

The General frowned. He was afraid he was going to be disappointed in this boy.

"And so," went on Jimmy, "if you would give me a nickel for car-fare, I think we might call it square."

The General fumbled around for his eye-glasses, put them on, and looked at Jimmy in astonishment.

"A nickel?" he asked.

"Yes, sir"; Jimmy blushed. "You know I ought to get back."

"Well, well," said the General. The boy had certainly the instincts of a gentleman. Not a single plea of poverty, and yet one could see that he was poor, very poor.

"THEN THE GENERAL, WITH KNIFE UPRAISED, STOPPED IN HIS CARVING OF THE COLD ROAST CHICKEN, AND TURNED TO JIMMY"

Just then a gong struck softly somewhere. "I'm not going to let you go until you have a bit of lunch with us," said the General. "I have told my wife of Jimmy of the market, and now I want you to meet her."

So Jimmy went down into a wonderful dining-room, where the silver and the cut glass shone, and where at the farther side of the table was the sweetest little old lady, who came and shook hands with him.

Jimmy had never before eaten lunch where the soup was served in little cups, but the General's wife put him at his ease when she told him that his very own soup-bunches were in that soup, and if he didn't eat plenty of it he wouldn't be advertising his wares. Then the General, with knife upraised, stopped in his carving of the cold roast chicken, and turned to Jimmy with a smile of approval in his genial face, and said that it was his sage, too, that was in the chicken dressing.

They made Jimmy talk, and finally he told them of his ambition for a basket stall.

"And when do you expect to get it?" asked the General, with a smile.

"When I get the goose that lays the golden egg, I am afraid, sir," said Jimmy, a little sadly.

Then the General's wife asked questions, and Jimmy told her about the Little Mother, and of their life together; but not one word did he tell of their urgent need, for Jimmy had not learned to beg.

At last the wonderful lunch was over, somewhat to Jimmy's relief, it must be confessed.

"I shall come and see your mother, Jimmy," said the General's wife, as Jimmy left her.

Out in the hall the General handed the boy a nickel. "Business is business, young man," he said, with a twinkle in his eye.

———————————

That night Jimmy and his mother sat up very late, for the boy had so much to tell.

"Do you think I was wrong to ask for the nickel, Mother?" he asked anxiously, when he had finished.

"No," said his mother; "but I am glad you didn't ask for more."

Then, after Jimmy had gone to bed, the mother sat up for a long time, wondering how the rent was to be paid.

On Easter Monday morning Jimmy and the Little Mother started out to pick the arbutus and the early violets which Jimmy was to sell Tuesday at his little stall.

It was a sunshiny morning. The broad road was hard and white after the April showers, the sky was blue, and the air was sweet with the breath of bursting buds. And, in spite of cares, Jimmy and his mother had a very happy time as they filled their baskets.

At last they sat down to tie up the bunches. Carriage after carriage passed them. As the last bunch of flowers was laid in Jimmy's basket, a victoria drawn by a pair of grays stopped in front of the flower-gatherers.

"Well, well," said a hearty voice, and there were the General and his wife! They had called for Jimmy and his mother, they said, and had been directed to the wooded hill.

"Get in, get in," commanded the General; and, in spite of the Little Mother's hesitancy and timid protests, she was helped up beside the General's wife by the footman, while Jimmy hopped in beside the General, and away they went over the hard white road.

The General was in a gay mood.

"Well, my boy, have you found your golden egg?" he asked Jimmy.

"No, sir," said Jimmy, gravely; "not yet."

"Too bad, too bad," said the old gentleman, while he shifted a white box that was on the seat between himself and Jimmy to the other side.

"You're quite sure, are you, that you could only get it from a goose?" he asked later.

"Get what, sir?" said Jimmy, whose eyes were on the gay crowds that thronged the sidewalks.

"The egg," said the General.

"Oh—yes, sir," replied Jimmy, with a smile.

The General leaned back and laughed and laughed until he was red in the face; but Jimmy could see nothing to laugh at, so he merely smiled politely, and wondered what the joke was.

At last they reached Jimmy's home, and the General helped the Little Mother out. As he did so he handed her a white box. Jimmy was busy watching the gray horses, and saw nothing else.

"For the boy," whispered the General.

The Little Mother shook her head doubtfully.

"Bless you, madam," cried the General, testily, "I have a boy of my own—if he *is* six feet two in his stockings." Then, in a softer tone, "I beg of you to take it, madam; it will please an old man and give the boy a start."

So when good-by had been said, and Jimmy stood looking after the carriage and the prancing grays, the Little Mother put the white box in his hand.

Jimmy opened it, and there on a nest of white cotton was an egg. But it was different from any of the eggs that Jimmy had sold on Saturday. It was large and gilded, and around the middle was a yellow ribbon.

Jimmy lifted it out, and found it very heavy.

"What do you think it is?" he said.

"Untie the ribbon," advised his mother, whose quick eyes saw a faint line which showed an opening.

Jimmy pulled the yellow ribbon, the upper half of the egg opened on a hinge, and there were glistening gold coins—five-dollar gold pieces.

"Oh!" said Jimmy, and he sat down on the step, breathless with surprise and joy.

A slip of white paper lay between two of the coins. Jimmy snatched it out, and this is what he read:

Please accept the contents of the golden egg, with the best wishes of —

THE GOOSE.

ARBOR DAY

No uniform date in the different States

Arbor Day is a designated day upon which the people and especially the school children plant trees and shrubs along the highways and other suitable places. It was first observed in Nebraska. The State board of agriculture offered prizes for the counties and persons planting the largest number of trees, and it is said that more than a million trees were planted the first year, while within sixteen years over 350,000,000 trees and vines were planted in the State.

This custom, so beautiful and useful, spread rapidly, and now is recognized by the statutes of many of the States.

The exact date naturally varies with the climate.

THE PLANTING OF THE APPLE-TREE

By William Cullen Bryant

Come, let us plant the apple-tree,
Cleave the tough greensward with the spade;
Wide let its hollow bed be made;
There gently lay the roots, and there

Sift the dark mold with kindly care,
And press it o'er them tenderly;
As 'round the sleeping infant's feet
We softly fold the cradle-sheet,
So plant we the apple-tree.

What plant we in this apple-tree?
Buds, which the breath of summer days
Shall lengthen into leafy sprays;
Boughs, where the thrush, with crimson breast,
Shall hunt and sing, and hide her nest;
We plant upon the sunny lea
A shadow for the noontide hour,
A shelter from the summer shower,
When we plant the apple-tree.

What plant we in this apple-tree?
Sweets for a hundred flowery springs
To load the May-wind's restless wings,
When, from the orchard-row, he pours
Its fragrance through our open doors;
A world of blossoms for the bee,
Flowers for the sick girl's silent room,
For the glad infant sprigs of bloom,
We plant with the apple-tree.

What plant we in this apple-tree?
Fruits that shall swell in sunny June,
And redden in the August noon,
And drop, when gentle airs come by,
That fan the blue September sky;
While children come, with cries of glee,
And seek them where the fragrant grass
Betrays their bed to those who pass,
At the foot of the apple-tree.

And when, above this apple-tree,
The winter stars are glittering bright,
And winds go howling through the night,
Girls whose young eyes o'erflow with mirth
Shall peel its fruit by cottage-hearth,
And guests in prouder homes shall see,
Heaped with the grape of Cintra's vine,
And golden orange of the line,
The fruit of the apple-tree.

The fruitage of this apple-tree,
Winds and our flag of stripe and star
Shall bear to coasts that lie afar,
Where men shall wonder at the view,
And ask in what fair groves they grew;
And sojourners beyond the sea
Shall think of childhood's careless day,
And long, long hours of summer play,
In the shade of the apple-tree.

Each year shall give this apple-tree
A broader flush of roseate bloom,
A deeper maze of verdurous gloom,
And loosen, when the frost-clouds lower,
The crisp brown leaves in thicker shower.
The years shall come and pass, but we
Shall hear no longer, where we lie,

The summer's songs, the autumn's sigh,
In the boughs of the apple-tree.

And time shall waste this apple-tree.
Oh, when its aged branches throw
Thin shadows on the ground below,
Shall fraud and force and iron will
Oppress the weak and helpless still?
What shall the tasks of mercy be,
Amid the toils, the strifes, the tears
Of those who live when length of years
Is wasting this little apple-tree?

"Who planted this old apple-tree?"
The children of that distant day
Thus to some aged man shall say;
And, gazing on its mossy stem,
The gray-haired man shall answer them:
"A poet of the land was he,
Born in the rude but good old times;
'Tis said he made some quaint old rhymes
On planting the apple-tree."

APRIL FOOLS' DAY

April 1

So old is the custom of playing amiable and harmless tricks upon the first of April that its origin is not definitely known. It is not a holiday and not worthy to be one, but it should be good for our sense of humor and that is one of the best things we can have. An April fool is sometimes called a "Fourth-month Dunce."

FOURTH-MONTH DUNCE

By H.M.M.

The curious custom of joking on the first of April, sending the ignorant or the unwary on fruitless errands, for the sake of making them feel foolish and having a laugh at them, prevails very widely in the world. And whether you call the victim a "Fourth-month Dunce," an "April fool," an "April fish" (as in France), or an "April gowk" (as in Scotland), the object, to deceive him and laugh at him, is everywhere the same.

The custom has been traced back for ages; all through Europe, as far back as the records go. The "Feast of Fools" is mentioned as celebrated by the ancient Romans. In Asia the Hindus have a festival, ending on the 31st of March, called the "Huli festival," in which they play the same sort of first of April pranks—translated into Hindi,—laughing at the victim, and making him a "Huli fool." It goes back to Persia, where it is supposed to have had a beginning, in very ancient times, in the celebration of spring, when their New Year begins.

How it came to be what we everywhere find it, the wise men cannot agree. The many authorities are so divided, that I see no way but for us to accept the custom as we find it, wherever we may happen to be, and be careful not to abuse it.

Some jokes are peculiar to some places. In England, where it is called "All Fools' Day," one favorite joke is to send the greenhorn to a bookseller to buy the "Life and Adventures of Eve's Grandmother," or to a cobbler to buy a few cents' worth of "strap oil,"—strap oil being, in the language of the shoe-making brotherhood, a personal application of the leather.

But this custom, with others, common in coarser and rougher times, is fast dying out. Even now it is left almost entirely to playful children. This sentiment, quoted from an English almanac of a hundred years ago, will, I'm sure, meet the approval of "grown-ups" of this century:

"But 't is a thing to be disputed,
Which is the greatest fool reputed,
The one that innocently went,
Or he that him designedly sent."

MEMORIAL DAY

May 30

It is said that the observance of this day grew originally out of the custom of the widows, mothers, and children of the Confederate dead in the South strewing the soldiers' graves with flowers, including the unmarked graves of the Union soldiers. There was no settled date for this in the North until 1868, when General John A. Logan, as commander-in-chief of the Grand Army of the Republic, designated May 30. It is now generally observed, and is a legal holiday in most of the States.

[**Editor's Note:** The Uniform Holidays Act established Memorial Day as a federal legal holiday, fixed on a Monday, beginning in 1971. All 50 states observe the holiday.]

THE BOY IN GRAY

A Ballad for Memorial Day

By Mary Bradley

Fredericksburg had had her fray,
And the armies stood at bay;
Back of wall, and top of hill,
Union men and men in gray
Glowered at each other still.

In the space between the two
Many a hapless boy in blue
Lay face upward to the skies;
Many another, just as true,
Filled the air with frantic cries.

"Love of God!" with pity stirred,
Cried a rebel lad who heard.
"This is more than I can bear!
General, only say the word,
They shall have some water there."

"What's the use?" his general,
Frowning, asked. "A Yankee ball
Drops you dead, or worse, half way,
Once you go beyond the wall."
"May be!" said the boy in gray.

"Still I'll risk it, if you please."
And the senior, ill at ease,
Nodded, growling under breath,
"For his mortal enemies
I have sent the lad to death."

Then a hotter fire began
As across the field he ran, —
Yankee shooters marked a prey, —
But beside each wounded man
Heedless knelt the boy in gray.

Parched lips hailed him as he came;
Throats with fever all aflame,
While the balls were spinning by,
Drained the cup he offered them,
Blessed him with their dying cry.

Suddenly, through rain of those
Pattering shots, a shout uprose;
Din of voices filled his ears;
Firing ceased, and eager foes
Made the welkin ring with cheers.

"BUT BESIDE EACH WOUNDED MAN
HEEDLESS KNELT THE BOY IN GRAY"

Foes they were, of bitter need,
Still to every noble deed
Hearts of men, thank God, must thrill;
And we thrill, too, as we read
Of those cheers on Marye's Hill.

Days of battle long since done,
Days of peace and blessing won,
Better is it to forget
Cruel work of sword and gun:
But some deeds are treasures yet.

While a grateful nation showers
Graves of heroes with her flowers,
Here's a wreath for one to-day:
North or South, we claim him ours—
Honor to the Boy in Gray!

FLAG DAY

June 14

The first recognition of Flag Day by the New York schools was in 1889, but it is now generally observed by appropriate exercises. June 14 is the anniversary of the adoption of the Stars and Stripes by the Continental Congress in the year 1777. This was the flag which, first raised over an American vessel by John Paul Jones, became the emblem of the new republic. In some places another day is set apart instead.

THE STARS AND STRIPES

By Henry Russell Wray

While every lad and lassie in the land knows and has read all about the famous old Liberty Bell, too little is known of the origin and growth of America's dearest emblem—her flag. William Penn's city—Philadelphia—is gemmed with many historical landmarks, but none should be more dear to us than that little old building still standing on Arch street, over whose doorway is the number — 239. For in a small back room in this primitive dwelling, during the uncertain struggle for independence by the American colonies, was designed and made the first American flag, known as the "Stars and Stripes," now respected and honored in every quarter of the world, and loved and patriotically worshiped at home.

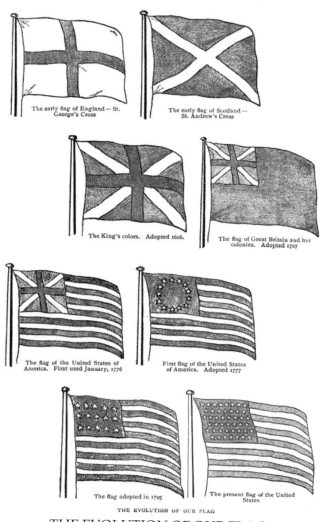

THE EVOLUTION OF OUR FLAG

The early history of our great flag is very interesting.

It is a matter of record that during the early days of the Revolution the colonists made use of flags of various devices.

It is nowadays generally accepted as a fact that the final idea of the Stars and Stripes as a national flag was borrowed from or suggested by the coat of arms of General George Washington's family.

The first definite action taken by the colonies toward creating a flag, was a resolution passed by Congress in 1775, appointing a committee of three gentlemen—Benjamin Franklin and Messrs. Harrison and Lynch—to consider and devise a national flag. The result of the work of this committee was the adoption of the "King's Colors" as a union (or corner square), combined with thirteen stripes, alternate red and white, showing "that although the colonies united for defense against England's tyranny, they still acknowledged her sovereignty."

NUMBER 239 ARCH STREET,
PHILADELPHIA — THE HOUSE IN WHICH
THE FIRST "STARS AND STRIPES" WAS MADE

The first public acceptance, recognition, and salute of this flag occurred January 2, 1776, at Washington's headquarters, Cambridge, Massachusetts. The name given to this flag was "The Flag of the Union," and sometimes it was called the "Cambridge Flag." The design of this flag was a combination of the crosses of St. George and St. Andrew in a blue field in the upper left-hand corner, bordered by thirteen stripes for the thirteen colonies.

But in the spring of 1777 Congress appointed another committee "authorized to design a suitable flag for the nation."

This committee seems to have consisted of General George Washington and Robert Morris. They called upon Mrs. Elizabeth Ross, of Philadelphia, and from a pencil-drawing by General Washington engaged her to make a flag.

This flag, the first of a number she made, was cut out and completed in the back parlor of her little Arch street home.

It was the first legally established emblem, and was adopted by Congress June 14, 1777, under the act which provided for stripes alternately red and white, with a union of thirteen white stars in a field of blue. This act read as follows: "Resolved, That the flag of the United States be thirteen stripes, alternate red and white: that the union be thirteen stars, white in a blue field, representing a new constellation."

FOURTH OF JULY

This is the greatest secular holiday of our country, its observance being sanctioned by the laws of every State. The birthday of our liberty would be a hard one to fix, but by common consent the anniversary of the signing of the Declaration of Independence is the one observed. The use of powder to celebrate the day is gradually going out on account of the large number of lives annually lost through accidents. It is known officially as Independence Day.

A STORY OF THE FLAG

By Victor Mapes

When the Fourth of July came, we had been abroad nearly two months, and during that time I think we had not seen a single American flag. On the morning of the Fourth, however, we walked out on the Paris boulevards, and a number of flags were hanging out from the different American shops, which are quite frequent there. They looked strange to us; and the idea occurred to Frank, for the first time, that the United States was one of a great many nations living next to one another in this world—that it was his own nation, a kind of big family he belonged to. The Fourth of July was a sort of big, family birthday, and the flags were out so as to tell the Frenchmen and everybody else not to forget the fact.

A feeling of this nature came over Frank that morning, and he called out, "There's another!" every time a new flag came in view. He stopped two or three times to count the number of them in sight, and showed in various ways that he, America, and the American flag had come to a new understanding with one another.

During the morning, Frank's cousin George, a boy two or three years older than Frank, who had been in Paris the preceding winter, came to our hotel; and, as I had some matters to attend to in the afternoon, they went off together to see sights and to have a good time.

When Frank returned about dinner-time, and came up to the room where I was writing letters, I noticed a small American-flag pin stuck in the lapel of his coat.

"George had two," he said in answer to my question; "and he gave me this one. He's been in Paris a year now, and he says we ought to wear them or maybe people won't know we're Americans. But say, Uncle Jack, where do you think I got that?" He opened a paper bundle he had under his arm and unrolled a weather-beaten American flag.

"Where?" asked I, naturally supposing it came from George's house.

"We took it off of Lafayette's tomb."

I opened my eyes in astonishment; while he went on:

"George says the American Consul, or the American Consul-General, or somebody, put it on the tomb last Fourth of July, for our government, because Lafayette, don't you know, helped us in the Revolution."

"They ought to put a new flag on every year, George says," explained Frank, seeing my amazement, "on Fourth of July morning. But the American Consul, or whoever he is that's here now, is a new man, George thinks; anyhow, he forgot to do it. So we bought a new flag and we did it.

"There were a lot of people at the tomb when we went there, and we guessed they were all waiting to see the new flag put on. We waited, too, but no soldiers or anybody came; and after a while the people all went away. Then George said:

"'Somebody ought to put on a new flag—let's do it!'

"We went to a store on the Boulevard, and for twenty francs bought a new flag just like this old one. George and I each paid half. There were two women and a little girl at the tomb when we got back, and we waited till they went away. Then we unrolled the new flag and took the old one off the tomb.

"We thought we ought to say something when we put the new flag on, but we didn't know what to say. George said they always made a regular speech thanking Lafayette for helping us in the Revolution, but we thought it didn't matter much. So we just took off our hats when we spread out the new flag on the grave, and then we rolled up the old flag and came away.

"We drew lots for it afterward, and I'm going to take it back home with me.

"Somebody ought to have done it, and as we were both American boys, it was all right, wasn't it?"

Right or wrong, the flag that travelers see on Lafayette's tomb this year, as a mark of the American nation's sentiment toward the great Frenchman, is the one put there by two small, self-appointed representatives. And the flag put there the year before, with fitting ceremony by the authorized official, Frank preserves carefully hung up on the wall of his little room in America.

Also Available From Better Days Books

Games *for* Hallow-e'en

BY MARY F. BLAIN

First published in 1912, this vintage holiday classic is packed with ideas and activities guaranteed to make your Victorian-themed Halloween gathering the most authentic, impressive and talked about party of the year! Includes instructions for more than 60 traditional Halloween games, plus dozens of riddles, party game "forfeits" and more!

View the Complete Better Days Books Catalog
Of Quality Vintage Reprint Editions at
www.BetterDaysBooks.com

Also Available From Better Days Books

CHOCOLATE AND COCOA RECIPES
By Miss Parloa
And
HOME MADE CANDY RECIPES
By Mrs. Janet Mckenzie Hill

(Complete In One Volume)

Compiled for complimentary distribution by chocolate maker Walter Baker & Co., Ltd. in 1909, *Chocolate And Cocoa Recipes By Miss Parloa And Home Made Candy Recipes By Mrs. Janet Mckenzie Hill* gives detailed instructions for creating 139 Victorian Era chocolate delicacies ranging from the simplest hot breakfast cocoa to the most extravagant desserts and elegant party dishes and delights. A must-own collectible volume for lovers of chocolate, vintage cook books and American Victoriana alike!

View the Complete Better Days Books Catalog
Of Quality Vintage Reprint Editions at
www.BetterDaysBooks.com

Also Available From Better Days Books
MY BOOK OF INDOOR GAMES

BY CLARENCE SQUAREMAN

The perfect "cabin fever" companion for energetic children cooped up indoors during the long winter months - or in urban settings where outdoor play is unsafe or unsavory year round - Clarence Squareman's 1916 classic *My Book Of Indoor Games* shares rules and clear play instructions for nearly 200 games, puzzles, riddles and tricks with which children of all ages can actively and intelligently amuse themselves without need for computers, video game play systems or TV. Many of these games are so old as to have been long forgotten by present generations - allowing them to be rediscovered and made "new again" by children today. A great "idea book" for homeschool groups, teachers, child care staff or anyone who truly cares about caring for children, *My Book Of Indoor Games* is your child's ticket to unending imaginative fun. The vintage cover and numerous interior illustrations make this book a great nostalgia piece for grown-ups, as well!

Also Available From Better Days Books

The American Frugal Housewife

By Mrs. Lydia M. Child

Originally published in 1832, this extraordinary manual for the homemaker of modest means is far more than a mere "cookbook." In an age before electricity, refrigeration or any other modern convenience, the fine art of storing, preparing and serving food presented difficulties unimagined in our time, challenges our forebears mastered with ingenuity, hard work, the inherited knowledge of generations past, and the sheer American pluck required to make the cheerful best of any social or economic situation. Also included are instructions for making soap, beer and wine, for repairing worn clothing and furniture, for enduring poverty, and even for rightly educating one's daughters. A rich treasure trove of practical frontier knowledge, Lydia M. Child's *The American Frugal Housewife* is an essential volume for contemporary homesteaders, antiquarian collectors, and anyone who longs for a firsthand taste of real American history.

Discover Better Days and Better Ways with *Better Days Books!*

Better Days Books publishes quality reprint editions of classic American non-fiction books, focusing on titles that uniquely capture the spirit of the 18th, 19th and early 20th Centuries – times when courage, self-reliance, clean living and upright moral virtue defined the common character of the American People. In making these classic works available to a new generation, it is our hope that many will rediscover and be inspired to express in their own lives a bit of the historic "*can-do!*" attitude and unflinching strength of character which lie squarely at the root of our rich American heritage, but which have been sorely lacking from our national identity since the "Cultural Revolution" of the 1960s. At *Better Days Books*, we dedicate our efforts to restoring our nation's lost fortitude and to preserving our irreplaceable heritage of traditional skills and knowledge against the onslaught of technology, for the enjoyment and edification of Americans today, and of many generations yet to come. May our best days lie ahead!

View The Complete Catalog of *Better Days Books*
Vintage American Reprint Editions at
www.BetterDaysBooks.com

Made in the USA
Middletown, DE
22 February 2023

25395463R00064